A Skills Based Approach to Drawing

Drawing
is a Class Act

Years 1–2

Meg Fabian

'In learning to draw (unlike learning to write) you learn to look.'
'Then you teach yourself to see and to feel what you see.'
David Hockney
from the forward to Draw:
How to Master the Art by
Jeffrey Camp

Brilliant Publications

Acknowledgements

I would like to thank:
Andrew Riley, Primary Phase Adviser and erstwhile Headteacher at two of the primary schools where I have taught art, for his help, advice, encouragement and inspiration not only in the initial stages of this book but also during all the time we worked together.

Dr Aubrey Wilson for his sterling advice and support.

Chris Wightman and Phil Creek, the Devon Curriculum Services Art Advisers, for all the art courses they have run, when I have turned up exhausted and jaded and left enthused and full of ideas.

I would also like to thank the following primary schools for their permission to include in the publication examples of work by children in their schools. This work has been done over a number of years. Wherever work is named, permission was sought for inclusion.

Primary schools
Burrington
Chawleigh
Clovelly
East Worlington
Filleigh
Winkleigh
Witheridge

Individual pupils
Alex Lyons-Martin
Andrew Loat
Anna Marie Searle
Annabel Squire
Archie Muirhead
Billie Reay
Chloe Gregory
Coralie Thomson
Daisy Barker
Daisy Burt
Daisy Waldron
Ebony Thorne
George Porter
Harriet Gregory
Jade Tanton
Joe Blackford
Joe Witheridge
John Widlake
Jonathan Slacke
Jordan Wild
Laura Dennis
Lauren Thornton
Miranda Sherlock
Natasha Elder
Nicky Loat
Philip Searle
Sam Jeffrey
Sarah Vanstone
Scott Warren
Shane Sexon
Shona Gregory
Simone Charles
Stephen Grimshire
Taylor-Anne Harrington
Thomas Corras
Thomas Ellis
Tom Vanstone
Victoria Rawlings
Wesley Knowler
William Taylor-Jones

The publishers and author would like to thank the following for permission to reproduce artwork in this book:

Design and Artists Copyright Society (DACS) (105); Kunsthistorisches Museum, Vienna (64, 110); Charles and Josette Lenars/CORBIS (104); Musee Royaux des Beaux Arts, Brussels (22, 103); National Gallery of Victoria, Melbourne (105); Windsor Castle (16, 102)

The publishers apologise if they have inadvertently miscredited anyone for any of the works of art used in this book. We will correct any mistakes pointed out to us as soon as feasible.

Brilliant Publications, 1 Church View, Sparrow Hall Farm, Edlesborough, Dunstable, Bedfordshire LU6 2ES
Tel: 01525 229720
Fax: 01525 229725
e-mail: info@brilliantpublications.co.uk
website: www.brilliantpublications.co.uk
The name Brilliant Publications and the logo are registered trademarks.

Written by Meg Fabian
Illustrations supplied by class pupils (see list above)
Front cover design by Lynda Murray
Cover illustrations by Daisy Waldron, John Widlake, Jordan Wild, Miranda Sherlock and Shona Gregory

© Meg Fabian 2005
ISBN 1 903853 60 5 (978-1-903853-60-3)
Printed in the UK by RMP Print & Design
10 9 8 7 6 5 4 3 2 1

Forward

Many of the examples in this book have been developed through collaborative work across a number of small primary schools in Devon. The schools worked with Meg Fabian over a period of two years. This collaborative work, involving a specialist with a passion for her subject, was instrumental in raising children's standards and confidence in drawing. Teachers also benefited from gaining knowledge and skills to improve their own understanding and teaching of drawing.

It became clear during the collaborative work that teachers needed the guidance and encouragement of a subject specialist: this is what this book provides for all teachers. By clearly setting out the development of drawing skills from the beginning, offering guidance on progression in learning and providing ideas to support classroom activities, this book is exactly what busy primary teachers need.

The schools involved in this innovative collaborative work believed in the importance of raising standards in art and the impact this has on the promotion of high standards in other subjects of the curriculum and, importantly, in children's self-esteem and confidence. The schools reflected this belief in practice and dedicated a higher proportion of time to the teaching of art. They also recognized that, to achieve high standards in art, the class teacher may need support in identifying the developmental stages of drawing.

This is where this book will be an invaluable resource.

David Chaplin
Lead Adviser
Devon Curriculum Services

Year 2 child's drawing of motifs and patterns from Russian artefacts

Contents

A skills-based approach to drawing

The aim of this book is to support non-specialist art teachers working in primary schools. It is intended for teachers who say, *'I want to help my children get better at drawing but I don't know how,'* and to help teachers respond confidently to all those children who say, *'I'm rubbish at drawing.'*

This book is designed to be easily accessible. It is intended that teachers can glance at a page, read the title, look at the example of pupils' work and know what to do without reading all the text. Teachers wanting further information can read the page.

Each lesson plan includes:
- ❏ Lesson title indicating the skill or technique being covered
- ❏ Logo indicating the type of lesson:

- ❏ Time needed to complete lesson
- ❏ Resources
- ❏ Links to National Curriculum programmes of study
- ❏ Introduction to pupils
- ❏ Practical activity
- ❏ Examples of pupils' work.

Many lessons also include:
- ❏ Background information necessary to deliver the lesson
- ❏ Examples of works of art that illustrate the use of the skills being taught.

Some lessons include:
- ❏ A photocopiable worksheet

How the skills-based approach works

The principle of this book is that the skills and techniques covered should be used for a purpose as soon as possible. It is important that children have the opportunity to use their skills in a drawing context.

For this reason a 'Using skill' lesson follows each 'Key Skill' or 'Skill' lesson throughout the book. For example, when children have learned the skills for using line with charcoal they can then use these skills to draw school buildings, windswept trees, etc. This also gives the teacher a clear focus for assessment.

The drawing subject could be linked to another appropriate topic, for example if the local environment is being studied in history or geography, then this is an excellent opportunity to apply the art skills to drawing landscape.

For some lessons it is recommended that teachers demonstrate or model basic techniques. This generally involves nothing more challenging than drawing light and dark lines using charcoal or drawing a cube on the board. Paper can be fixed to the board with Blu-tac® for demonstrating. Where paper is necessary for teacher modelling, it is mentioned in the resources list for that lesson.

Many of the skills exercises will result in a piece of work that is visually pleasing in its own right. Children will produce something they can be proud of. This factor has been deliberately built in. Very often, once the skill has been taught, the pieces of work can be adapted or mounted to produce a stunning piece of artwork that can be displayed to great effect. There are some good examples of this in the 'Playing around with line' lesson (see page 33). If it makes the children feel *'Wow, I did that',* it will increase their confidence, their self-esteem and their willingness to take the next step.

The skills-based approach doesn't inhibit creativity; it helps children to know how to create certain effects. If they have increased control and understanding of the different media, they will be able to experiment with more confidence and be empowered to express themselves.

What the book covers

This book covers all the National Curriculum programmes of study related to drawing. The programmes of study are listed for each lesson.

The book has chapters on line, tone, texture, pattern, looking, figures and faces, and chalk and charcoal. The contents pages clearly set out the lessons for each chapter, giving the type of lesson and approximate time needed for each. There is also a chapter on evaluation and assessment.

The book:
- ❑ Clearly sets out the progression of skills to be taught at Key Stage 1
- ❑ Gives examples of how the skills can be applied (children are more motivated when they can see clearly how the skill can be used)
- ❑ Has carefully planned lessons which are ideal for single age classes where there is a wide range of ability and for small schools with mixed age ranges
- ❑ Has examples of pupils' artwork for every lesson
- ❑ Has a section of photocopiable sheets that relate to various lessons (to be found at the back of the book).

It is not expected that all the lessons will be delivered. Teachers can teach one, some, or most of the lessons. However, if there is very limited time, then it is suggested that just the key skill lessons are taught.

These lessons are marked with this symbol:
The key skill lessons appear in bold on the contents pages.

Other books in the series
This book is one of a series of three. The other books in the series cover Key Stage 2:

Years 3–4   ISBN 1 903853 61 3 (978-1-903853-61-0)
Years 5–6   ISBN 1 903853 62 1 (978-1-903853-62-7)

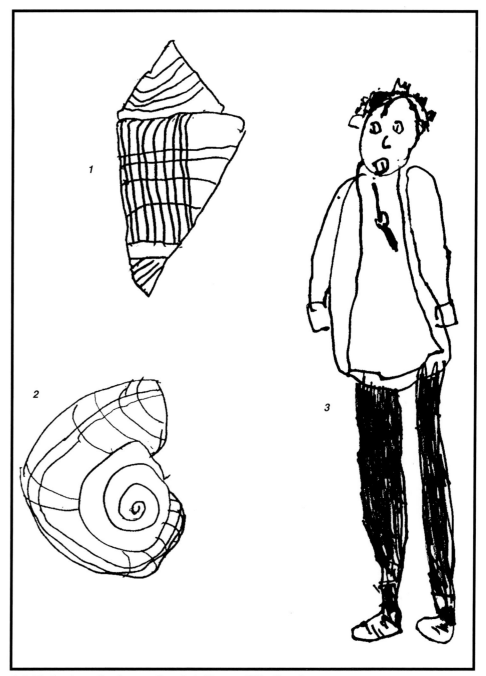

1–2: Taylor-Anne Harrington, Year 2; 3: Thomas Ellis, Year 1

About drawing

Dictionary derivation of 'to draw':

- Old High German   Tragen
- Old High Norse   Draga
- Old High Goth   Gadragon
- Old English   Dragon

The various ways we use the word 'drawing' are fascinating, at once connected and yet different:

- To draw out
- To be drawn along
- To be drawn into
- To draw alongside
- To draw on experience
- To draw closer …

'It is the *draw closer* that is the most interesting. When I am drawing, I become totally involved, I concentrate intensely, become more closely involved with what I am drawing. There comes a point when I am almost at one with my subject, I feel all my senses are engaged. I miss nothing.'
Meg Fabian, the author

So many adults feel that they cannot draw; this is perhaps because they have never been taught to draw.

'Most adults in the Western world do not progress in art skills beyond the level of the development they reached at nine or ten. In most mental and physical activities individuals' skills change and develop as they grow to adulthood. The development of drawing skills, however, seems to halt unaccountably at an early age for most people. This could be because drawing is not a vital skill for survival in our culture, but reading and writing are.'
Betty Edwards, Drawing on the Right Side of the Brain

Learning to draw is something that never stops. Children are surprised when they hear that artists go on learning and getting better all their lives, that they never consider they have stopped developing as artists.

Drawing is surrounded by mystique. It is commonly imagined that the few who can perform its magical rites have been invested with a divine gift – but actually anyone can learn to draw.

'From the age of six, I had a mania for drawing the form of things. At seventy-five I learned a little about the real structure of nature. At ninety I shall penetrate the mystery of things; at a hundred I shall have reached a marvellous stage; and when I am a hundred and ten, everything I do, be it a dot or a line, will be alive.'
Written at the age of 75 by Owakio Rojin, an old man mad about drawing (from Betty Edwards, Drawing on the Right Side of the Brain)

There are many purposes for drawing, for example recording, expressing, communicating and analyzing.

This book is about exploring the media and elements.

About looking

The key to drawing is in the looking. For this reason a separate chapter is devoted to it.

Children find it hard to believe that as artists their eyes are more important than their hands. The skills covered in the Looking chapter will help them understand how and why this is true. They will be guided not only to look closely but to look with purpose and to develop different ways of looking.

'In developing children's ability to see and understand various visual situations you produce a storehouse of ideas that can be used in countless different ways.'
Ian Simpson, Drawing, Seeing and Observation

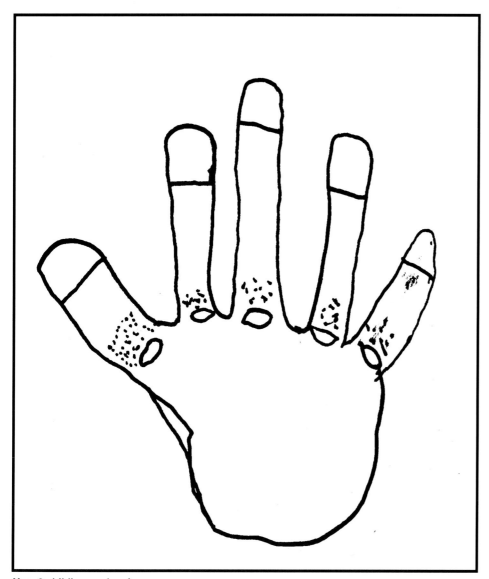

Year 2 child's pen drawing

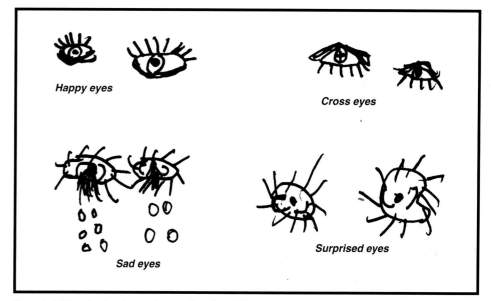

Year 1 children's drawings of eyes showing different expressions

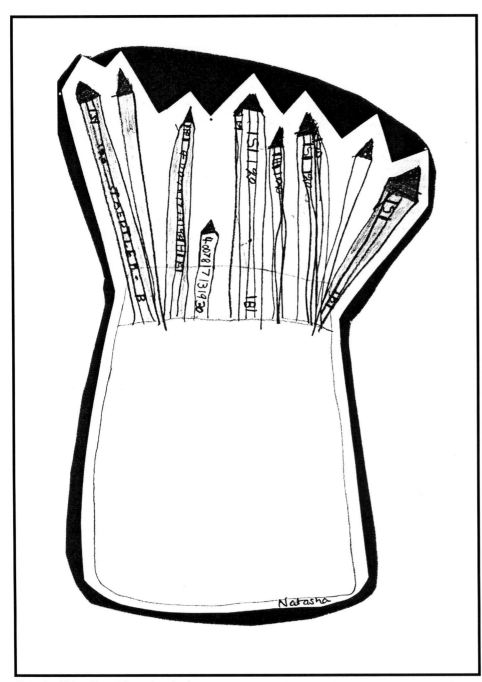

Natasha Elder, Year 2 (pen drawing)

Range of media

To deliver the lessons in this book you will need (absolute basics are in bold):

☐ One set of drawing pencils H to 8B (for display)
☐ B, **2B** and 4B **pencils**
☐ **Fine line pens (tip size 0.4 mm)**
☐ Permanent pens, medium tip
☐ Permanent pens, broad tip (round tips are more manageable than chisel)
☐ **Charcoal, medium thickness**
☐ **White chalk** or white chalky pastel
☐ **Fixative** (see Glossary – cheap hairspray can be used)
☐ **Oil pastels**
☐ Coloured felt tips, different thicknesses
☐ Ball-point pens
☐ Brusho (powdered watercolour)
☐ Coloured pencils, art quality
☐ Crayons
☐ Sketchbooks, A4 (A3 only if you have *plenty* of table space!)
☐ Viewfinders (see Glossary and page 64)
☐ Magnifying glasses
☐ Mirrors (plastic)
☐ Cartridge paper (see Glossary)

Starting-out kit:

Tip: buy good-quality media, topping up when you can. Gradually extend your range a little at a time.

- ❐ B and 4B pencils (add 2B when you can)
- ❐ Fine line pens (tip size 0.4 mm), water-based
- ❐ Permanent pens, broad tip (add medium tip when you can)
- ❐ Charcoal, medium thickness
- ❐ Fixative (see Glossary)
- ❐ Oil pastels (extend range of colours later)
- ❐ Art pastels (chalky)
- ❐ Art quality coloured pencils. (These are expensive so could be left until budget allows. The water colour pencils are the most versatile as they can be used in two ways: as coloured pencils and as a form of water colours.)
- ❐ Sketchbooks, A4 (A3 only if you have *plenty* of table space!)
- ❐ Viewfinders made from cut black sugar paper (replace with card or corrugated plastic when you can)

> 'Drawing is the discipline by which I constantly rediscover the world. I have learned that what I have never drawn I have never seen, and when I start drawing an ordinary thing, I realize how extraordinary it is, sheer miracle.'
> Frederick Frank, The Zen of Seeing

> 'For me drawing is a kind of thinking, but it is also about the medium.'
> Antony Gormley, sculptor of The Angel of the North, (from his book, Drawing)

A well-resourced art cupboard could have:

- ❐ H, B, 2B, 4B, 6B pencils
- ❐ Fine line pens (tip size 0.4 mm), water-based
- ❐ Fine (tip size 0.4 mm), medium and broad permanent pens
- ❐ Charcoal, medium thickness
- ❐ Fixative (see Glossary)
- ❐ Oil pastels, 25 colours, bright and subtle, extra white and black
- ❐ Art pastels, good range of colours, including landscape colours
- ❐ Conté crayons (soft pastels) black, white, earth colours, sepia, burned sienna, etc.
- ❐ Good-quality crayons, some sets in people colours
- ❐ Art quality coloured pencils, landscape and portrait sets
- ❐ Water colour pencils
- ❐ Graphite
- ❐ Metallic crayons
- ❐ Metallic pens – fine and broad
- ❐ Sketchbooks with heavy quality paper
- ❐ Clipboards for outside drawing
- ❐ Black plastic viewfinders
- ❐ Magnifying glasses with flexible necks that clamp onto desk
- ❐ Lamps with flexible necks
- ❐ Collection of reproductions of works of art, filed according to topic or subject, or QCA art documents
- ❐ CDs of reproductions of works of art for use on computer or white board
- ❐ Collection of artefacts for drawing (see list on page 61)

Sketchbooks

> 'Drawing sketches is like planting seeds in order to get pictures later.'
> *Vincent van Gogh, in a letter to his brother Theo (from The Letters)*

Most artists use a sketchbook. It is a vital part of their equipment used to collect visual information and to record ideas and feelings. On his death Picasso left 178 sketchbooks, containing a huge variety of ideas recorded over a period of 60 years.

It is a good idea for children to see artists' sketchbooks and to hear how they use them. This could be part of a school visit by a practising artist. If this is not possible, members of a local art group would probably be willing to visit the school and allow the children to see their sketchbooks and answer children's questions about how they are used.

Throughout this book it is suggested that children do the work outlined in each lesson directly in their sketchbooks. Sketchbooks are listed in the resources list for most lessons. When it is not possible to work directly in the sketchbooks (for example, in the Chalk and charcoal chapter the drawings are executed on mid-tone sugar paper), the drawings could be stuck into the sketchbooks later.

A sketchbook is a wonderful record of a child's development as a young artist. Being able to look back at their work and see their progression raises children's self-esteem.

Teachers can write comments in sketchbooks just as they would in other subject books. Comments should be specific, for example: *'I like the way you have used different kinds of lines in this drawing,'* or *'I can tell that you were looking very carefully when you drew this.'*

Sketchbooks can be started in Key Stage 1, and should carry on through the school. They should be at least A4 and of reasonable quality paper. A3 sketchbooks take up a lot of table space and, unless the class is very small or the classroom/art room very spacious, they are rather unwieldy. Slightly bigger than A4 is ideal, as A4 paper can be stuck in without any overlaps. Work may often be done on loose paper and stuck in later, perhaps because the artwork is going to be displayed or work has been done on different types or colours of paper.

The sketchbook paper needs to be thick enough to take paint, as the sketchbooks should be used across the whole art curriculum. The paper should have slight texture, as very smooth paper is not ideal for pencil.

The covers should be stiff enough for the children to lean on when drawing outside.

> 'A day passed without drawing is a day wasted.'
> *Antony Gormley, sculptor of The Angel of the North (from his book, Drawing)*

Sketchbooks can be used for different purposes:

- ❏ Collecting visual information
- ❏ Capturing an image
- ❏ Planning
- ❏ Trying out new skills
- ❏ Experimenting with media
- ❏ Visual storytelling
- ❏ Note-taking
- ❏ Designing
- ❏ Describing
- ❏ Storing ideas
- ❏ Recording research
- ❏ Recording investigations
- ❏ Recording responses
- ❏ Recording trips and visits
- ❏ Recording a visual diary

Sketchbooks are:

- ❏ A record of achievement
- ❏ A record of development

They can be used for assessment:

- ❏ Self-evaluation
- ❏ For reporting to parents
- ❏ As evidence

Sketchbooks are a source of inspiration.

Wesley Knowler, Year 2 (a variety of lines in pencil)

Erasers and rulers

Rulers

For most drawing, children do not need rulers. Lines drawn with rulers tend to be similar so the resulting drawings are often without life and character. If pupils become dependent on rulers, they miss the opportunity to develop their ability to draw straight lines.

Erasers

Erasers create far worse problems. Although erasers may be used when areas of dark charcoal need to be lifted, to help create contrast and depth, the rest of the time they create more problems than they solve.

If children have used erasers in previous art classes there are usually cries of indignation when their use is banned. Tell them that erasers destroy the surface of the paper, and further drawing on that surface is not as effective. Repeated rubbings out tend to crease the paper and look messy, and heavy lines never rub out cleanly and always leave a grubby patch.

Some children may rub out almost everything they do and end up with little to show for their efforts.

Most important of all is the fact that, if children think they can rub something out, they tend not to approach the task with as much thought and observation as they should. They are more likely to launch into the drawing without those few extra moments of close looking and intense observation. They are inclined also to place the drawing on the paper without much forethought, secure in the knowledge that they can rub it out.

Whilst enthusiasm and a desire to get started are wonderful, they must be weighed up against the value of deep thought and close looking. A good balance of both is ideal.

If they cannot use an eraser, they will need to be that bit more thoughtful and observant, and this is what will help them to progress.

Explain all this to them as it helps if they understand that the ban on erasers is better for their own artistic development.

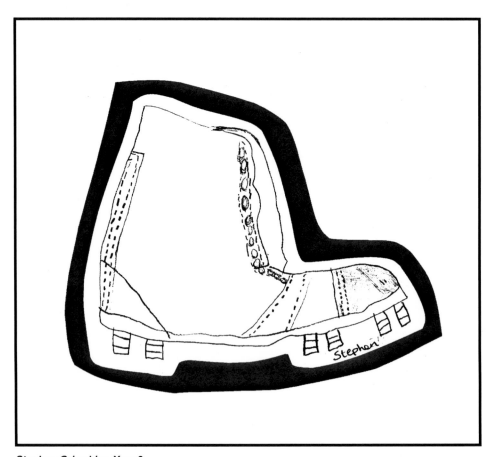

Stephen Grimshire, Year 2

Line

Andrew Loat, Year 2 (line drawings of shells)

Year 2 child's pen doodle

Rationale

Children's exploration of different lines in different media will enable them to use a range of lines in their own work. These activities will open their eyes to the huge variety of lines that they can use.

Children learning to draw lines soon discover that they are gaining control over a most powerful tool.

The simplest line suggests direction, divides space, and has length, width, tone and texture. It can enclose or define shape, and can suggest contour. It is with line that we create writing.

There are no limits to the possibilities of pencil. It is the most basic tool in the art of drawing, and also one of the most versatile.

Drawing light lines

This is one of the areas that create the most problems for children in drawing. The business of starting a drawing using light lines, so that you can alter them if necessary, is a very difficult one for children to grasp. The ability to draw light lines is not relevant in narrative drawing with younger pupils, but it becomes increasingly more important as children try to achieve a particular result.

Explaining to children why light lines are important

❑ Explain that when artists start out on a drawing they don't expect for one minute that they will get everything right first time. So they use light lines or marks that they can alter later if they need to.

❑ Children could be told, *'You have to start a drawing somewhere and you can't be sure you won't have to change something, so make it easier for yourself: start off with light lines. You can then put in the lines that you think are better over the light lines.'*

❑ Remind them that erasers often make a mess of the page. Show some examples of drawings by artists that show lines which have been drawn over, or next to, other lines. Leonardo da Vinci's drawings are an excellent example. See Resource sheet 1 (page 102) which

'Study for the Trivulzio Monument' by Leonardo da Vinci, showing use of light lines (a larger photocopiable version appears on page 102). Reproduced with permission from Windsor Castle

has an enlarged version of the drawing shown on page 16. Tell the children that he was a genius who worked as an artist for a very long time. He changed his drawings as he went along. The children will almost certainly want to change something too so they should avoid using very dark lines as it is much harder to change them.

☐ Say, for example, *'Leonardo didn't throw down his pencil when his drawings went wrong, saying, "I give up, I'm rubbish at drawing."'* Try to take the pressure off the children to feel they must get it right first time.

Different ways to help children use light lines
Try inviting someone who can draw (it doesn't have to be an artist) to draw in front of the children, thinking out loud as the drawing progresses, altering things as they go along. It's better if the person isn't too accomplished, as making the children feel daunted would be counterproductive.

It helps if children understand that it is the amount of pressure on the pencil that results in the darkness of the line. Try asking them to close their eyes, make a line on the paper and then guess how dark it will be. Then ask them to make three more lines, each darker than the first, then three lighter ones. Look to see how well they have judged the darkness and lightness of the lines.

You could try referring to light lines as whispering or secret lines.

I talked to one newly qualified teacher whose class had produced some stunning drawings; you could clearly see light lines beneath the final ones. When I asked her how she had achieved this, she replied, *'Easy, I just gave them 2H pencils for the initial drawings, then 2B to improve and complete them.'* Then she added, *'If they do dark lines to begin with, I just tear the drawings up!'* Her first idea is worth a try.

About this chapter
In this chapter children make their own line collections for future reference. They use the skill they have learned in a context. They experiment in a range of media, and investigate the use of line by other artists.

If you are short of time, do just the key skill lessons.

Year 2 child's drawing using line and tone

George Porter, Year 1 (a variety of lines in pencil)

KEY SKILL

Making different types of line in pencil

Time	Resources	National
30 min.	Sketchbooks	**Curriculum**
	2B pencils	2a, 4a
	1 set of drawing pencils H to 8B, if you have them	
	Large piece of white paper for teacher modelling	

Introduction
'We are going to make lots of different lines with 2B pencils. Using lots of different lines will make your drawings even better. The B on the pencil means black. The more Bs the pencil has, the blacker the line it will make. The H stands for hard.'

Practical activity
Lines
❏ Show them the set of drawing pencils if you have them. Demonstrate the variations in tone they make.

❏ Demonstrate making each type of line. Ask the children to work in their sketchbooks to create the following:
  * A short, straight line
  * A short, straight, darker line next to it
  * A short, straight, lighter line
  * A long, straight line
  * A long, straight, darker line next to it
  * A long, straight, lighter line.

❏ Repeat with wavy lines, zigzags, broken lines, wiggly lines, etc. Children usually have plenty of suggestions.

- Introduce drawing lines with the side of the pencil lead. Model this, to help them get the correct angle of the lead against the paper. It should be flat against the paper. The pencil needs to have a decent length of lead, or the children will be not be able to make a wide line.
- Children then try making some of the other types of line with the side of the pencil.

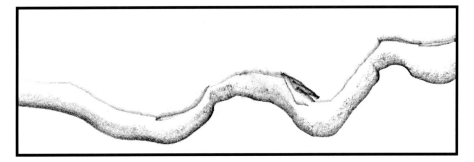

Dots and dashes

- Explain that dots and dashes are really short lines and they can be very useful for creating certain effects.
- Children draw light dots, dark dots, dots close together and dots far apart.
- Repeat with dashes.
- Ask what they think the dots and dashes would be useful for. They will usually suggest rain, grass or animal fur.

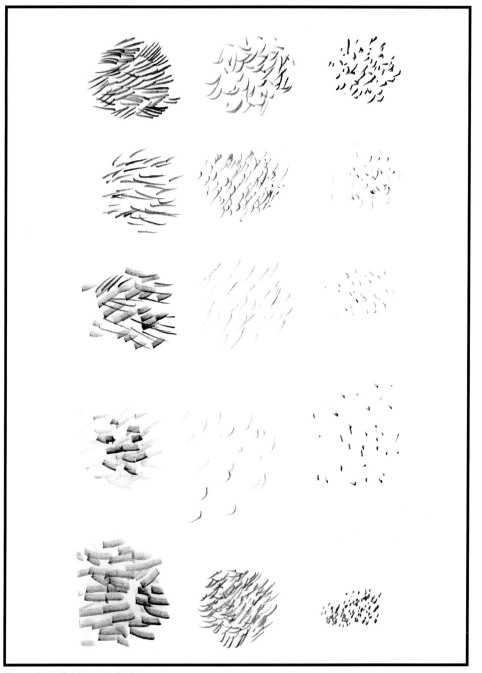

Examples of dots and dashes

Years 1 and 2 children's pencil drawings using a variety of lines

 USING SKILL

Drawing lines in pencil

Time	Resources	National
30 min.	Sketchbooks/paper	**Curriculum**
	2B pencils	1a, 2b, 3a, 3b
	Artefacts (see text below and list on page 61)	

Introduction

'Now you have tried out lots of different lines with your 2B pencils, you are going to do some drawings using as many of those lines as you think will look good. I will be looking at your drawings and hoping to see lots of different kinds of lines.'

Remind them to use the side of their pencil as well as its point, and not to forget light and dark lines.

Ideas for subject matter

❏ Draw outside – the school field, wild area or anywhere where there is scope to use lots of lines.
❏ Draw each other – lots of scope here with hair, eyelashes, freckles, folds in clothes, etc.
❏ Draw artefacts – plants, soft toys, feathers.

Suggest the children look back in their sketchbooks to remind themselves of all the different lines they have drawn.

Page 21 can be photocopied and used as an assessment activity. Before asking the children to draw a picture in the empty box, review the following expectations with them:

❏ All children will be able to draw lines with pencil.
❏ Most children will use a number of different lines when drawing with pencil.
❏ A few children will be able to use line to create particular effects.

Name _____

Date _____

Success criteria as explained to children

❒ You **must** include more than one kind of line with your drawing.

❒ You **should** use lots of different lines.

❒ You **could** create the effect of fur, fabric, shadow etc. by using different kinds of lines.

These criteria should really be drawn up with the pupils as the skill is being taught. Children can use the success criteria to make judgements about their work, followed by teacher judgements. For further information on success criteria see page 94.

'Boats on the Sea' by Vincent van Gogh with viewfinder placed on top. Resource sheet 2 (page 103) contains a larger copy of this work of art. Reproduced with permission from Musee Royaux des Beaux Arts, Brussels

 TRY THIS IDEA!

Looking at line in works of art

Time	Resources	National
15 min.	Resource sheet 2 (page 103) between two children, or photocopies of other drawings by van Gogh (see www.vangoghgallery.com) Viewfinders (see Glossary and page 64)	**Curriculum** 4c

Introduction
'We are going to take a close look at some drawings by van Gogh. You will be able to see that he has used lots of different lines to create different effects: fields, waves, grass, clouds. With a partner, be line detectives and see how many different kinds of lines you can find.'

Practical activity
❏ Give the children at least one copy of Resource sheet 2 and one viewfinder between two.
❏ Ask them to slide the viewfinder over the picture and talk about the lines they can see framed inside it.
❏ Ask them to look at different areas of the picture.

This is a good opportunity to brainstorm words that describe lines. Make a list that can be copied from the board or photocopied and stuck in their sketchbooks.

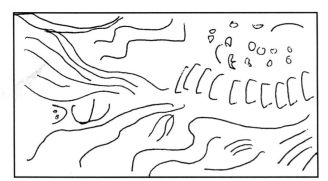

Lines found include curly, dotty, short and wavy ones

Background information
Van Gogh's drawings are an excellent resource for a line investigation. He used an amazing number of different kinds of lines. The drawings were mostly done in pen and ink. They were often preliminary drawings for paintings.

SKILL

Experimenting with line in different media

Time 45 min.	Resources Sketchbooks 2B (any B will do) pencils Crayons Chalky pastels Oil pastels Broad and fine pens Ball-point pens Felt tips, different thickness Charcoal	National Curriculum 2a

Introduction

'Do you remember making lots of different lines in pencil?' Show some of the work they did on that occasion. *'Lines can be made with many different media other than pencil: chalks, felt tips, ball-point pens, even paint. Today we are going to see what other types of line we can make.'*

Practical activity

❐ Put some of each media on every table and encourage the children to see how many different kinds of line they can make with each sort.

❐ Remind them they can achieve different effects using the side and the points of whatever they are using.

❐ Children can refer back to this page in their sketchbooks at a later date when they need to make decisions about which media would be the most effective for a particular subject.

Daisy Burt, Year 2

23

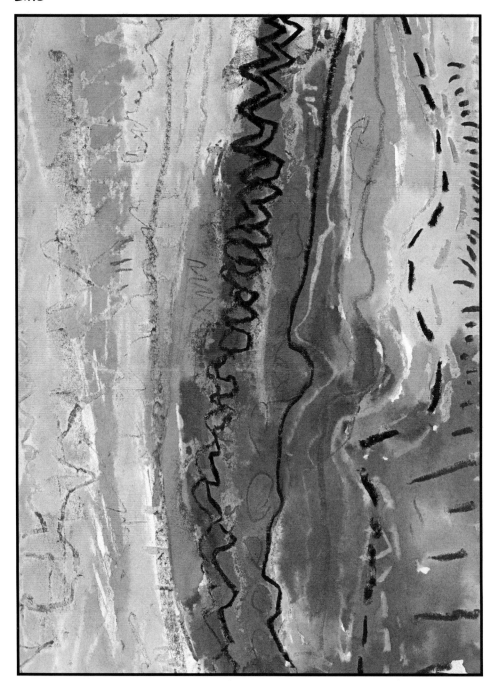

Sam Jeffrey, Year 1 (a variety of line marks in different media)

 USING SKILL

Mark-making with mixed media

Time	Resources	National
45 min.	Oil pastels	Curriculum
	Permanent pens, fine or broad	2a
	Ball-point pens	
	Crayons	
	Medium size brushes	
	Brusho (see Glossary) made up in bright colours	

Introduction
'We have made lots of different kinds of lines in different media. Lovely pictures can be made by using different media together.'

Activity
❐ Set out a wide selection of media on each table, but not the Brusho.

❐ Place the paper either landscape or portrait way round.

❐ Make different types of lines all the way across: a row of zigzags then a row of broken lines, a row of wavy lines and so on, using different types of media.

❐ Make as many different kinds of lines, in different colours and different media.

❐ When the page is covered, paint wide lines, using Brusho, in different colours, on top of the drawn lines.

❐ The pages make effective covers for their sketchbooks, or a colourful display.

Pens

Working in pen helps children create confident drawings. There is no possibility of rubbing out, and little opportunity to change lines. After some thought, they just have to launch into the drawing, knowing that what they put down will have to stay.

Fine line pens are very useful for crisp, delicate or detailed drawings. 0.4 mm is the easiest to obtain. There are finer tips available, but these are more appropriate for older children in Years 5 and 6.

Medium tip pens range from the average felt tip up to about 0.8 mm.

Broad pens could be anything from 1.6 mm upwards. The round tip is more manageable for Key Stage 1 than the chisel tip, as the children tend to forget which way to angle the point. Broad pens are good for large-scale or group work. They are also excellent for creating borders for large-scale pictures.

Lovely effects can be achieved by wetting water-based pen drawings with a damp fine brush. The black line goes a soft dark brown, and the lines blur a little. If the tip of a wet brush is touched against the lines the ink can be spread across a small area. This is known as bleeding or moving.

Permanent pens are very useful as paint or inks can be added to the drawings without the ink running. It is difficult to buy permanent fine pens, so the drawings can be photocopied and then paint added. Berol® make a double-ended permanent pen which has tips of two different thicknesses.

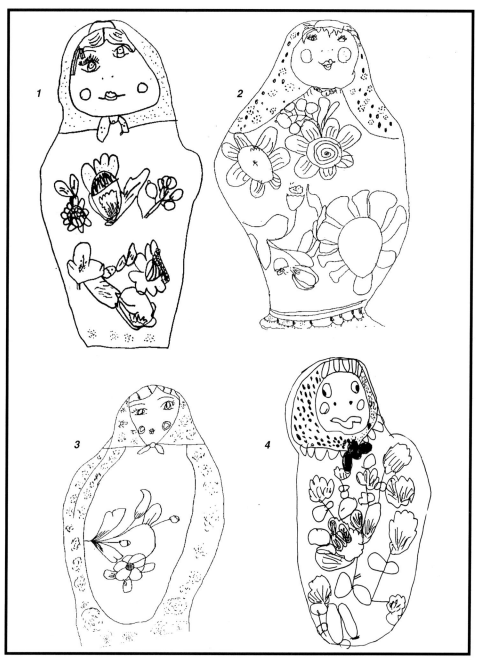

1: Archie Muirhead, Year 1; 2: Stephen Grimshire, Year 2; 3: Simone Charles, Year 2; 4: Philip Searle, Year 1 (see colour example by Miranda Sherlock on front cover)

Year 1 child's lines in three sizes of pen

 KEY SKILL

Making different lines with fine, medium and broad line pens

Time	Resources	National Curriculum
15 min.	Fine lines pens (approx. 0.4 mm) Medium tip pens Broad tip pens (round tip) Sketchbooks Resource sheet 2 (see page 103)	2a, 2b, 4a

Introduction
'We have found out how to make lots of different lines in pencil and other media. Today we are going to compare lines that different pens make.'

Practical activity
❐ Explain that different pens are good for different drawing tasks. Show them van Gogh's pen drawing of boats on the sea (Resource sheet 2) which demonstrates this well.
❐ Children look at different types of lines the artist has used.
❐ Using the same line types as in the lesson with pencils (see pages 18–19) children draw lines with each of the three different pens in turn.
❐ Elicit which pen would be good for drawing a piece of lace, a huge building and classroom furniture, etc.

Three sizes of pen

Time	Resources	National
45 min.	Broad, medium and fine line pens (black looks good) Resource sheet 3 (see page 104) A4 paper or sketchbooks	Curriculum 2a, 2b, 4a, 4c, 5a, 5d

Introduction
'Sometimes you can use more than one kind of pen in the same drawing. The different thickness of line can be very pleasing to the eye.'

Practical activity
❑ Put a selection of pens of different thicknesses on each table.
❑ Children put the paper portrait way round.
❑ Using the medium pen, they fill up the page with rectangles and squares of different sizes.
❑ They fill some of the shapes with smaller squares and rectangles.
❑ Show Resource sheet 3 which has some examples of African patterns. Point out the use of different thickness and lengths of line.
❑ Children draw windows and doors in some of the rectangles and squares.
❑ They fill in each shape with different straight lines, some with thick pens, some medium and some fine. Remind them to use broken lines, diagonal lines and crossing lines.
❑ Some shapes could contain a mixture of different thicknesses of pen lines.
❑ Children could add some palm trees over the top of the drawing to make it look like an African town.

Year 2 child's drawing of an African village using three sizes of pen (see colour example by Shona Gregory on front cover)

Year 1 child's drawing of settlements and pathways using broad pens

USING SKILL

Broad line pens

Time	Resources	National
45 min.	Sketchbooks or A3 paper	**Curriculum**
	Broad pens in two colours	2a, 4c, 5a
	Examples of Aboriginal artwork showing	
	pathways (see www.aboriginalartonline.com)	
	Resource sheet 4 (see page 105)	

Practical activity

❒ Show examples of Aboriginal artwork, including Resource sheet 4.

❒ Point out the pathways or routes between one place and another. The circles represent specific places and the lines are the routes.

❒ Children first draw circles dotted about their page. It is quite effective to use two colours, for example, brown and black.

❒ They draw a series of smaller circles inside them. If they have drawn small circles initially, ask them to draw larger ones around them.

❒ They then connect the circles with a number of parallel lines.

Medium line pens 1

Time	Resources	National
20 min.	Medium pens	Curriculum
	Sketchbooks or A4 paper	1a, 2a
	Selection of artefacts (could be large shells,	
	plants, branches, etc.) (see list on page 61)	

Introduction
'We are going to draw in medium pens today. These are very good for drawing larger things. You will find that you can add more detail than you can with broad pens.'

Practical activity
❏ Encourage the children to choose artefacts that lend themselves to bold outline drawings, for example: pots of pencils, large plants, doors and windows, computers, classroom furniture, the view from where they sit.
❏ Remind them that these are line drawings, so no solid colouring in.
❏ Children could complete two or three different drawings in the 20 minutes.

Background information
Drawing in pen helps to increase children's confidence. They have to launch into the drawing knowing they cannot change anything and 'go with the flow'.

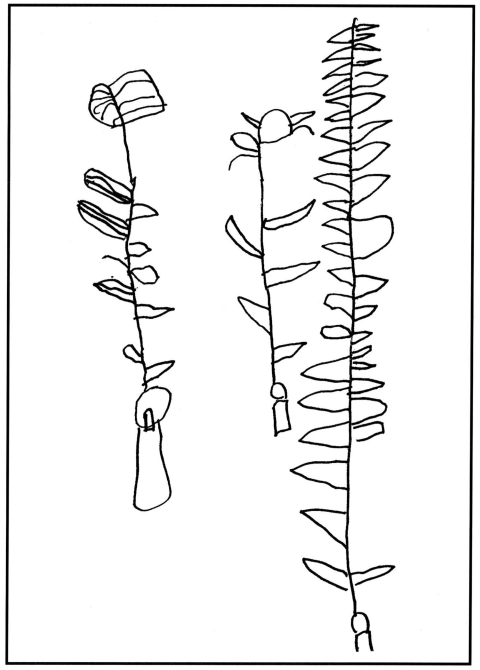

Tom Vanstone, Year 1 (line drawings in medium pen)

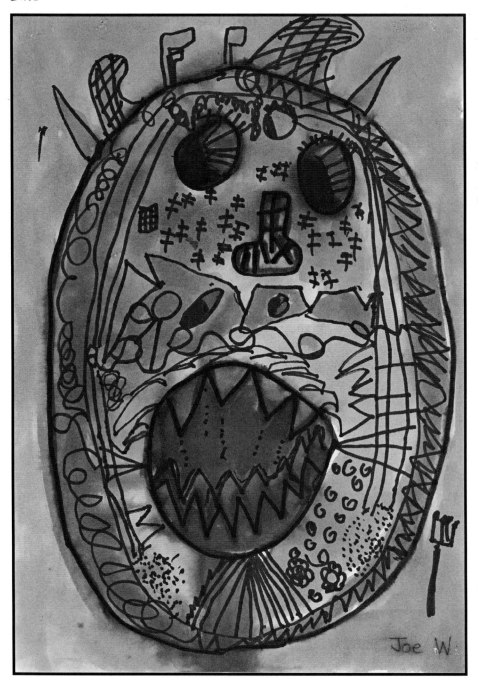

Joe Witheridge, Year 2 (drawing of mask using medium line pen and Brusho)

USING SKILL | Medium line pens 2

Time	Resources	National
45 min.	Medium pens (permanent)	**Curriculum**
	A4 paper	1a, 2a, 4c, 5a
	Sketchbooks	
	Brusho (see Glossary) red, yellow, brown	
	African masks and textiles and/or	
	Resource sheets 3 and 5 (pages 104 and 106)	
	Large piece of paper for teacher modelling	

Practical activity

❏ Show the masks and textiles, or pictures of them. Resource sheets 3 and 5 show African masks and patterns.

❏ Discuss all the shapes and patterns they can see.

❏ Draw some examples of patterns on your board or on A3 paper.

❏ Children draw their favourite masks in their sketchbooks.

❏ Then on paper (portrait way up) they draw a large mask of their own, that fills the page.

❏ They fill in the spaces with patterns and shapes they have found in the textiles and masks.

❏ Lastly, they paint over this with Brusho in warm colours.

Line drawing of mask

Fine line pens

USING SKILL

Time	Resources	National Curriculum
30 min.	Sketchbooks Fine line pens Selection of small artefacts to draw; could be flowers, grasses, seedheads, shells, or items linked to a topic (see list on page 61)	1a, 2a, 2b

Introduction
'Today we are going to draw with fine line pens. These are really good for doing careful, detailed drawings.'

Preparation for practical activity
❏ Explain that it is not a good idea to do solid colouring in with fine line pens as it wears down the tips quickly. You could say that they are called fine line pens because they are very good for drawing fine lines.
❏ Take at least five minutes to look at the artefacts (see Focusing looking through talking, page 62.)
❏ Draw attention to the shapes and patterns of the artefacts.
❏ Encourage children to view the items from different angles and to talk about what they can see (see example drawing on page 66).

Practical activity
❏ Children draw artefacts in their sketchbooks.
❏ After drawings are completed, you could ask them if they think they could have drawn these small detailed artefacts with broad or medium pens.

Further examples of children's work using fine line pens appear on page 32.

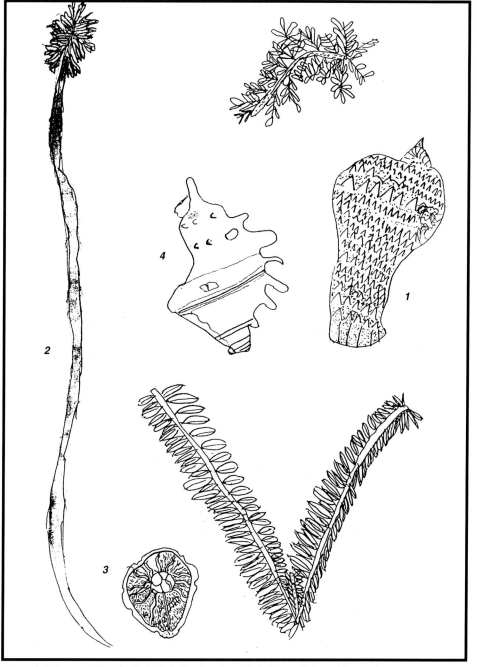

1: Harriet Gregory, Year 2; 2–4: Jade Tanton, Year 2 (other artists not known)

Daisy Waldron, Year 1 (pen drawing with water colour added on top, see colour example on front cover)

Wesley Knowler, Year 1 (doodle, see pages 52–53)

Playing around with line

Time	Resources	National
30 min.	Fine line pens	Curriculum
	A4 paper or sketchbooks	4a, 4c
	Large piece of white paper for teacher modelling	

Introduction

'Lines can create all sorts of illusions. They can give the impression of movement or solidness. They can also play tricks on your eyes.'

Practical activity

Teacher

❏ Demonstrate covering the paper with horizontal light wavy lines. This can be done on the board.
❏ Explain that the lines should follow the waves of the line above, like the grain in wood or moving water.

Children

❏ Draw wavy horizontal lines across the paper.
❏ Draw angled lines connecting the first two wavy lines.
❏ Connect the next wavy line with lines angled the other way.
❏ Continue down the page.

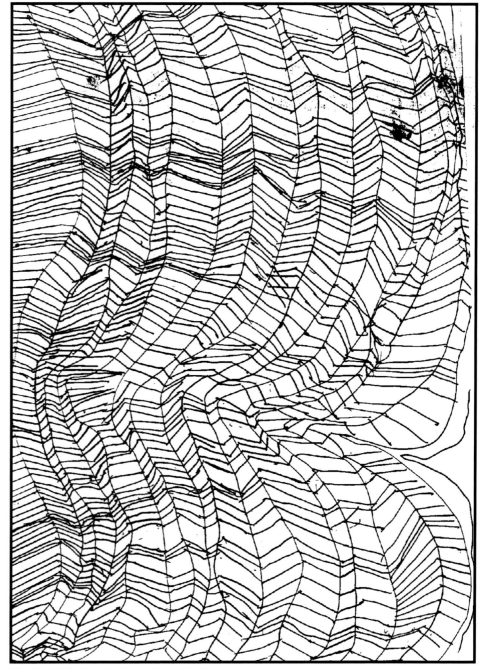

Year 2 child's line drawing using a fine line pen

Annabel Squire, Year 2

TRY THIS IDEA!

Scraper technique

Time	Resources	National
1 hour	Cartridge paper (see Glossary) no bigger than A5, or thin card Coloured crayons Oil pastels (optional) Cocktail sticks or paper clips (see note below)	**Curriculum** 1a, 2a

Introduction

'Today you are going to make line drawings by scraping away crayon instead of drawing with it.'

Practical activity

Teacher

❐ Show the picture on this page and explain how it was made (described below).

❐ Decide what subject matter children are going to do. Underwater pictures work well as do fireworks against a dark sky, or buildings at night. Handwriting patterns can look stunning. The children will need to have a fairly clear idea of their subject matter before they start, as it will affect the background colours.

Children

❐ Ask the children to cover their paper with a good layer of crayon. It doesn't matter which colour or how many colours.

❐ Repeat this using a black or dark oil pastel (these are softer than crayons and easier to apply).

❐ Using a cocktail stick, the children can scrape off a pattern or design to reveal the colours beneath. Paper clips with one end unwound make good scrapers.

Tone

Billie Reay, Year 1

Year 1 child's drawing using 4B pencil

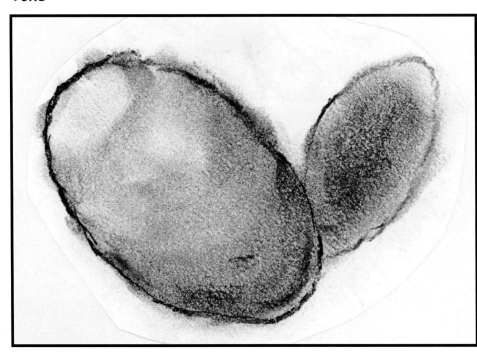

Year 2 child's charcoal drawing

'Light and shadows should blend without line or borders in the manner of smoke.'
Leonardo da Vinci,
Treatise on Painting

Rationale

The lightness or darkness of a colour, such as the shades of grey in the gradual change from black to white, is called tone.

Children can use tone to create the illusion of form and solidity, to create mood or to direct the viewer's attention.

Tone can make the whole effect of a drawing more dramatic and interesting.

The gradual transition of tone from light to dark was once regarded as essential to good drawing.

About this chapter

In this chapter children will learn how to make different tones in soft pencil and charcoal.

They will try to create the illusion of form and weight using different tones in pencil and charcoal.

They will then use this skill in a context.

The ability to shade meaningfully with a pencil is perhaps one of the most elusive aspects of drawing.

If you only have time for one skill, do the key skill first.

Year 2 child's feather drawing in pencil

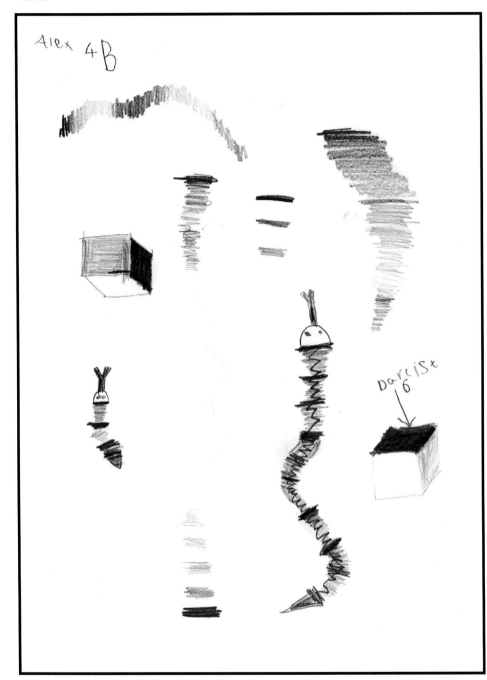

Alex Lyons-Martin, Year 2 (drawing of different tones in pencil)

 KEY SKILL ## Making different tones in pencil

Time	Resources	National
30 min.	Sketchbooks	**Curriculum**
	4B pencils	2a, 4a
	Large piece of white paper for teacher modelling	
	Fairly large black and white photograph from newspaper	

Introduction

'We are going to make different tones in soft pencil. Tone is the lightness or darkness of a colour, but we usually think of it as all the different shades between black and white.'

Remind the children that a black and white photograph will use all the different tones between black and white. Show the newspaper photograph.

Explain that using tone as well as line in drawing can help to make their drawings more exciting and interesting.

Practical activity

Teacher

- ❑ Model the different darkness of tone that can be made with a 4B pencil, by applying different pressures on the pencil.
- ❑ Explain that they can use both the side of the pencil and the point.

Children

- ❑ Children experiment with a range of different tones in their sketchbooks.
- ❑ They could make a 'Tone-y snake'. Ask them to change the tone as they draw the snake with the side of their pencils, then to add a head.
- ❑ Ask the children how they made the pencil create darker or lighter marks (more or less pressure).

☐ While they are doing this, quickly draw a cube on their page, as shown:

☐ Children shade in two surfaces, one medium and one dark. They can then see for themselves how tone creates the illusion of solidity.

Year 1 child's drawing of different tones in 4B pencil

Year 1 child's drawing using a range of tones

USING SKILL

Tones in pencil

Time	Resources	National Curriculum
30 min.	Sketchbooks 4B pencils Subject for drawing (see text below)	1a, 2a, 2b, 4a, 5b

Introduction

'Now you have tried to make different tones with your 4B pencils, you are going to do some drawings using tone as well as line. Tone will help to make your drawings look more solid, as if they have a thickness as well as a shape.'

Practical activity

❏ Almost any subject gives scope for including tone:
  * Inside: portraits, items in classroom, packed lunch boxes, history/science artefacts, pencil cases, soft toys
  * Outside: school buildings, gardens, view across the playground.
❏ Tell the children you will be looking at their drawings to see if they have used different tones.
❏ Before they begin drawing discuss which parts of the subject are the darkest, and which parts the lightest.
❏ Suggest they look back in their sketchbooks, to the page where they recorded their different tones, to remind them of the possible range in pencil.
❏ Children draw the subject first and then add the tones where they think appropriate.

SKILL ## Making different tones with charcoal

Time	Resources	National
15–20 min.	Sketchbooks	**Curriculum**
	Charcoal, medium thickness	2a, 4a
	Fixative (see Glossary)	
	Scrap paper	

Introduction
'Charcoal is made of burnt wood. It breaks easily but it makes wonderful dark marks on the paper. You can also make quite light marks, but what is really great about charcoal is that it smudges and you can make some lovely smoky effects. Today you are going to try out all the different tones you can make. Using tone helps to make the things you draw look more solid, as if they have weight and thickness.'

Practical activity
☐ Children make a very dark mark followed by one a little lighter and so on until the marks are so light they can hardly see them.

☐ Then try the same with the side of the charcoal. They can smudge some of the marks.

☐ While they are doing this, quickly draw a cube on their paper (see page 39).

☐ Ask them to shade one surface very darkly and one surface less darkly, leaving one side unshaded.

☐ Draw their attention to the three-dimensional effect.

Background information
Some children are wary of charcoal because it can be messy. You could point out that this is one of the plus points of charcoal, and that it dusts off hands easily. To make sure drawings are not spoiled by being leaned on as work progresses, provide the children with a piece of scrap paper that can be laid over any completed sections. Drawings can be sprayed with fixative at the end of the art session, when children have left the room.

Year 2 child's drawing of different tones in charcoal

Sam Jeffrey, Year 2

USING SKILL

Charcoal

Time	Resources	National
20–30 min.	Sketchbooks	Curriculum
	Charcoal, medium thickness, 3–4 cm pieces	1a, 2a, 4a, 5a
	Chalk	
	Scrap paper	
	Fixative (see Glossary)	
	Artefacts if drawing indoors (see list on page 61)	

Drawing outside or through a window is best as charcoal lends itself to landscape views such as trees or buildings. Alternatively, use artefacts such as black wellies, black and grey feathers, a black tape recorder or radio, black shoes. Place artefacts into groups, so each child will have a slightly different view as they sit round the table.

Introduction
'You have made lots of different tones in charcoal and now you are going to use charcoal and chalk to draw (whatever). *You are going to see if you can make these things look solid by using different tones in your drawings. You can give the appearance of depth by using chalk on the lightest part of your drawing and gently smudging/blending it into the charcoal.*

Practical activity
❏ Ask children to look at the subject. Discuss which is the darkest part of it, which the lightest, etc.
❏ Suggest that if they half close their eyes they might be able to see the darker and lighter areas more easily.
❏ Children start the drawing with a line outline, adding the tones later.
❏ Remind them of the different ways they can create tone: smudging or using different pressure to create light and dark tones.

Texture

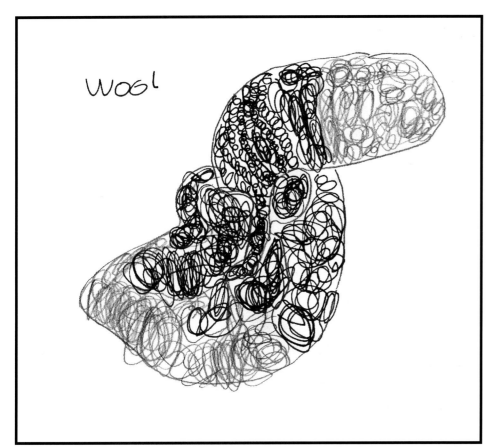

Wool

Year 2 child's drawing of textures of wool

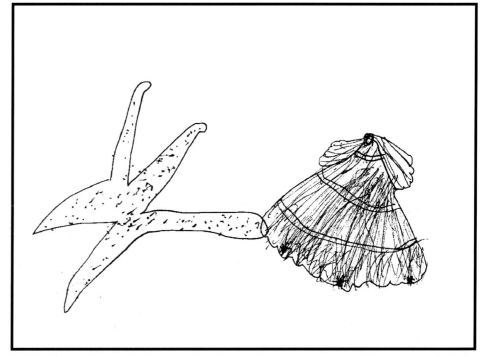

Year 1 child's drawing of textures on shells and starfish using fine line pen

Texture

Definition

The following definition can be given to children: Texture is the word that explains how things feel when we touch them. In drawing it is the marks made on a surface which represent the way textures look.

Textural surfaces are experienced through both touch and sight.

Rationale

Texture can add interest and definition to a drawing. Children can use drawn texture to create the illusion of difference between one surface and another, for example fur and skin, grass and stone.

Children can use texture to give their drawings variety and interest, to differentiate between one area and another, and to make their drawings visually more exciting.

About this chapter

In this chapter children will make a collection of marks, in different drawing media, to represent different textures. They will then use some of these in drawings done from first-hand observation.

Joe Blackford , Year 2 (drawing of textures on clothes)

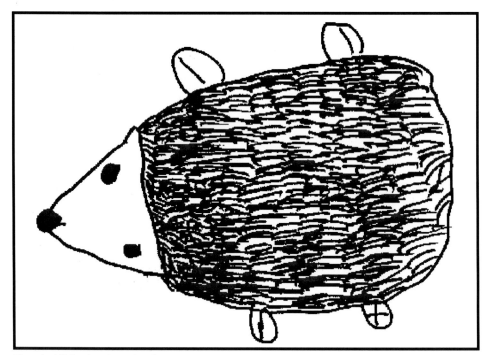

Year 1 child's drawing of soft toy mouse

Drawing different textures

Time	Resources	National Curriculum
30–40 min.	Sketchbooks Variety of drawing media, such as B or 2B pencils, felt tips, crayons, ball-point pens Collection of artefacts that have different textures: sandpaper, bark, fur, velvet, rough stone (see list on page 61) Feely bag to put artefacts in Large piece of white paper for teacher modelling	2a, 2b, 2c, 4a

Introduction

'Texture is a word that explains how things feel when we touch them. We can see lots of textures in nature, like feathers, bark or fur. Texture is all around us. On ourselves, our skin, our hair, our clothes – inside and outside our buildings. Our eyes give us information about the texture of things, but we can also feel them.'

Preliminary activity (oral)

❏ Play a 'feely' bag game by putting different textured objects in an opaque bag.
❏ Children close their eyes, feel inside the bag and describe what the textures feel like.
❏ Use their words to begin a texture word list; they could copy the list into their sketchbooks later.

Practical activity

❏ Give a collection of textured objects to the children.
❏ Allow them a few minutes to feel the items and talk about them.
❏ Divide a page in their sketchbooks into sections.
❏ Children make a series of marks in each section to represent the textures.
❏ Suggest they try different media. Model some marks, e.g. dots for sandpaper, little dashes for fur, scribbly lines for wool.

Background information

Texture is often introduced to children through rubbings. Rubbings are really a form of printing. This unit is about representing textures in drawing.

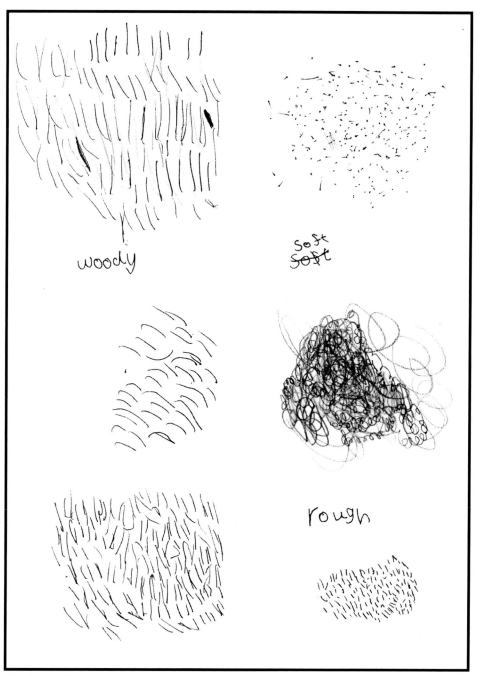

Alex Lyons-Martin, Year 2

Year 1 children's texture drawings

 USING SKILL

Drawing textures

Time	Resources	National
30 min.	Sketchbooks	**Curriculum**
	B or 2B pencils, ball-point pens and felt tips	1a, 2a, 2b, 4a,
	(all black if possible)	5a
	Artefacts with textured surfaces, e.g. knitted toys,	
	soft toys, shells, twigs with bark (see list on page 61)	
	Children could draw themselves or each other	

Introduction

'Different surfaces have different feels to them. If you feel your skin, your sweatshirt or the carpet, you will find they all have a different feel. These "feels" are called textures. Today you are going to try to create the way those textures look, using different types of pens and pencils.'

Practical activity

☐ Put a selection of different drawing media on the tables.

☐ Discuss the textures of the items to be drawn, and the media that would be most suitable for each subject matter. They might want to use more than one drawing medium within the same drawing to achieve a particular effect.

☐ Point out that one object might have more than one texture.

☐ Children first do a quick line drawing of the subject.

☐ Next they draw as many different textures as they can see, using whatever marks they think appropriate.

Background information

You may need to demonstrate how the children could represent fur, woven fabric or hair, for example, with different marks. If they are drawing themselves or each other, draw their attention to all the different textures: skin, different clothing materials, hair, etc. Point out that very short hair has a different texture from long or curly hair; that leather shoes have a different texture from fabric trainers. If the different drawing media are the same colour, they will find it easier to focus on the character of the medium.

Pattern

Year 2 child's drawing of her bedroom using fine line pen

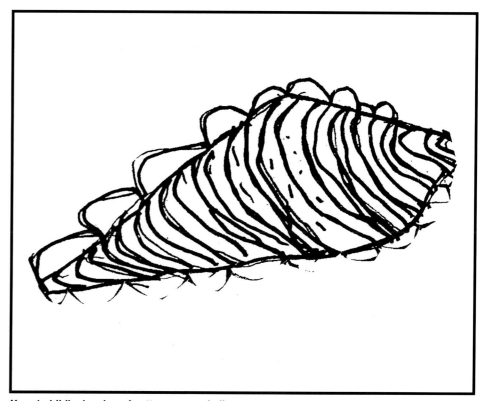

Year 1 child's drawing of patterns on a shell

Rationale

Pattern is an element of drawing that children tend to really enjoy. They can lose themselves in making patterns. They take pleasure in watching the lines and shapes gradually spread across the page. They feel a sense of achievement as the pattern develops, and while they are drawing they can day-dream a little. Day-dreaming is an essential element of creativity.

Investigating and making patterns is one way of developing their aesthetic sensibilities. In this chapter they will learn the basic elements of pattern and how to manipulate it. They will study both man-made and natural pattern, and develop their own.

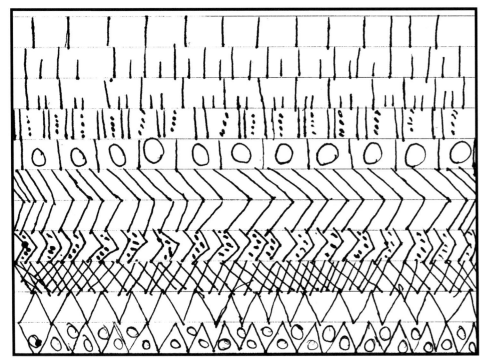

Daisy Waldron, Year 1

What is pattern?

Pattern is a repeat of lines shapes or colours. Pattern falls roughly into three groups: regular, irregular and unintentional pattern.

Pattern in nature, regular and irregular

Pattern in nature is often irregular, like the spots on a leopard. In the case of the leopard's spots or the tiger's stripes, there is a family of shapes. We perceive them as patterns but they are in fact irregular.

Other patterns in nature are regular in shape but they vary in size, such as the whorls on a tortoise shell, the scales on a fish or the feathers on a bird.

Single shapes such as the spiral on a shell can be taken and turned into a pattern. It can be the inspiration for a pattern, but on its own it is not a pattern.

Regular patterns

Regular patterns are more likely to be man-made. They are made by regular repeats of lines, shapes or colours.

The simplest pattern will consist of a single shape, line or colour, repeated in a regular way.

More complex patterns use more than one shape, line or colour. They might repeat in different ways, such as by rotating, reflecting or inverting motifs.

Unintentional pattern

Cars in a car park, books on shelves, leaves in a pile, products on supermarket shelves – because they are in families of shapes they create a kind of pattern.

Pattern for decoration

Pattern is closely associated with the decorative arts – tiles, pottery, fabrics, wall paper, tapestries, carpets – and also with folk art. From earliest time people have felt the need to decorate artefacts. Cultural traditions and fashions have defined styles, while materials and tools available have influenced the types of patterns produced.

Patterns are designed to fit the objects they are going to decorate; plate designs tend to be round, borders long and narrow.

Collecting, analyzing and creating patterns lead very naturally to print-making. Although in this chapter patterns will be drawn the work will still be a very useful foundation for printing.

About this chapter

Artists are inspired by pattern in nature, so it is a good starting point for children. We are surrounded by pattern in the natural and man-made world, so there is plenty of scope for stimulus.

In this chapter children will study how simple patterns can make line and shape.

They will study both regular and irregular patterns in nature, and those used in art and craft of different cultures.

They will develop a bank of patterns that they can later apply to designs.

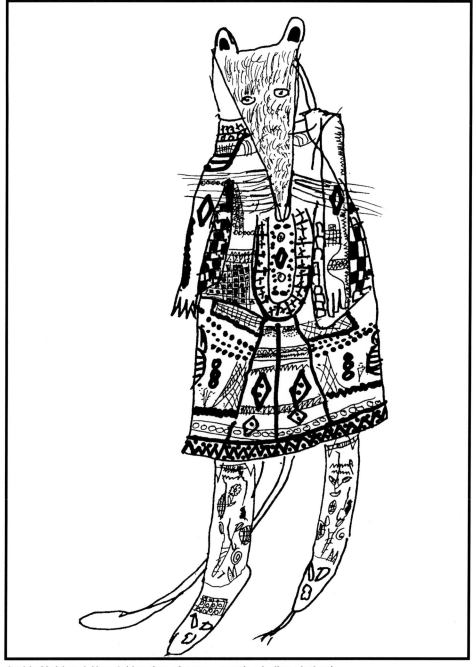

Archie Muirhead, Year 2 (drawing of mouse wearing Indian clothes)

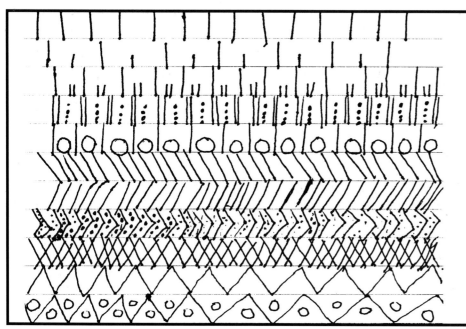
Ebony Thorne, Year 1

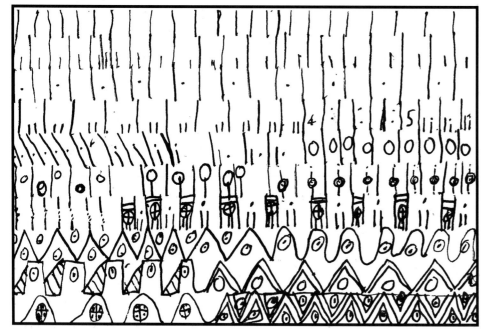
Lauren Thornton, Year 2

KEY SKILL

Making patterns with line

Time	Resources	National
30 min.	Sketchbooks	Curriculum
	Any pencil, HB will do (could use felt tips)	4a
	Large piece of paper for modelling	
	Resource sheets 6 and 7 (pages 107 and 108)	

Introduction
'Pattern is made up of repeated lines or shapes. You are going to make some simple patterns with lines.'

Practical activity
(Model each stage first.)

❑ Draw short straight lines, the same size and the same distance apart, across the paper:

| | | | | | | |

❑ Draw a long line, a short line, a long line, a short line and so on across the page:

| | | | | | |

❑ Next try a line and a dot, a line and a dot (tell them a dot is a tiny line).

| . | . | . | .

❑ Explain that it is important that the spaces between the lines should be the same size.

❏ There are many simple combinations they could try next. For example:

* two short lines, one long line and repeat

    || / || | || | || |

* two lines and two dots and repeat

    ||:||:||:   or ||••||••||••

* one line, one circle and repeat.

    | o | o | o

❏ They should now be able to make up some of their own.

Background information
This activity is closely related to handwriting and helps improve hand–eye co-ordination. Once they have grasped the concept of a pattern being a regular repeat, they can work on a smaller scale.

More able children could progress to the patterns on Resource sheets 7 and 8.

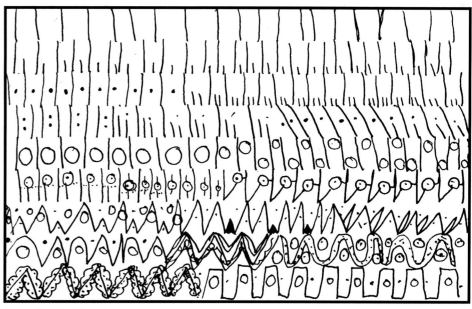

Laura Dennis, Year 2

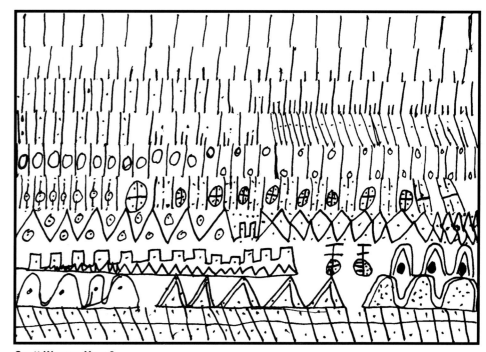

Scott Warren, Year 2

Pattern

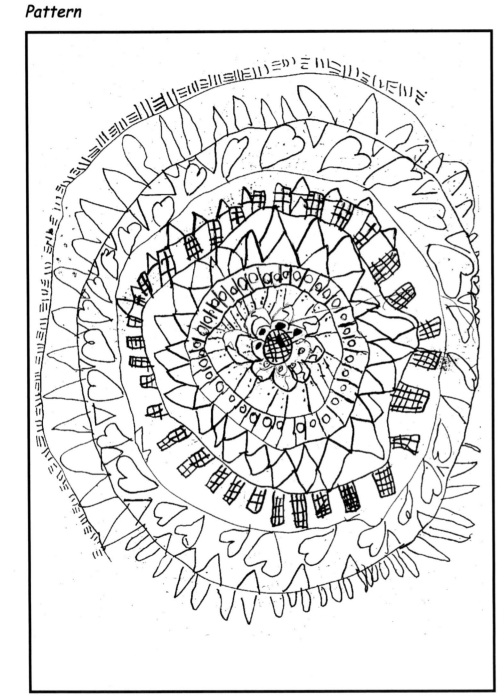

Year 1 child's doodle

USING SKILL

Using line patterns in a doodle

Time	Resources	National
15 min.	Sketchbooks/paper	**Curriculum**
to set up	Fine felt tips or fine line pens	4a
doodle	Resource sheet 8 (see page 109)	

Introduction

'Doodles can be a lot of fun to do. You will enjoy watching the patterns grow.'

Practical activity

❏ Show them some doodles done by other children. If none is available photocopy some examples from this book (e.g. these pages and Resource sheet 8).

❏ Explain that all these doodles started with a small shape in the middle and grew very very slowly over some weeks.

❏ Get the children to start the doodle in the middle of the paper with a simple shape such as a heart, cross, flower, square or circle.

❏ Add on to this motif different small lines and shapes, as below.

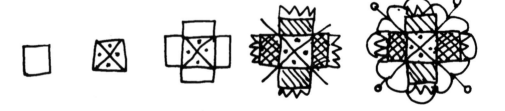

❑ Explain that every time their lines create a shape they should fill that shape in with a pattern. They can look back in their sketchbooks at the handwriting and line patterns they did in the previous activity for ideas.

❑ Remind them to work slowly and carefully.

❑ Once started, the doodles can be done in odd moments, for example clearing-up time or during registration.

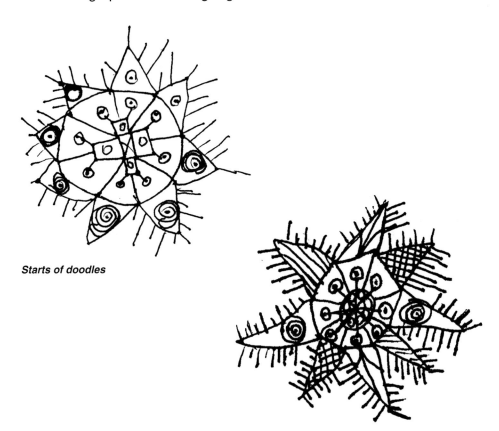

Starts of doodles

Background information

Children can build up their collections of line patterns over a period of time. They can then use them to decorate other pieces of work or they can turn the collections of patterns into works of art in their own right such as the doodles in this activity. Once children have a vocabulary of patterns they can launch into decorative art and craft activities with greater confidence.

Year 2 child's doodle

1: Laura Dennis, Year 1; 2: Harriet Gregory, Year 1 (other artists not known)

 TRY THIS IDEA!

Collecting patterns from nature

Time	Resources	National
30–40 min.	Sketchbooks	**Curriculum**
	B pencils	1a, 3b, 4a, 4b
	Selection of artefacts that have patterns: shells, leaves, fruit, vegetables, feathers (see list on page 61)	
	Magnifying glasses	
	Large piece of white paper for teacher modelling	

Introduction

'We can find lots of patterns in the world around us. Patterns are repeats of line, shapes or colours. You can see patterns in waves in the sea, clouds in the sky or in a tiny flower. These are natural patterns. Some patterns are made by people. Where can we see some examples of man-made patterns? Today, you are going to look very closely at some natural patterns, using magnifying glasses.'

Practical activity

- ❑ Distribute the artefacts so there is a variety on each table.
- ❑ Encourage children to talk about the patterns they can see. Model some of them on a piece of paper or the board – dots from the seedhead, some lines from the leaf and so on.
- ❑ Children draw the object and then draw just the pattern.
- ❑ The more able could label them, e.g. 'Pattern from inside an orange'.

Background information
Collections of patterns in sketchbooks are an invaluable resource. Children can use the patterns at some later time for decorating something, or for a project that is already in hand, for example: printing, indenting patterns on clay, or decorating a papier mâché plate.

'Much of learning to draw consists of discovering how things appear rather than how they are, and it is not until we begin to draw that most of us discover the tremendous difference between what we know about objects and what we see.'
Daniel Mendelowitz, *Drawing: A Study Guide*

John Widlake, Year 1 (spider's web)

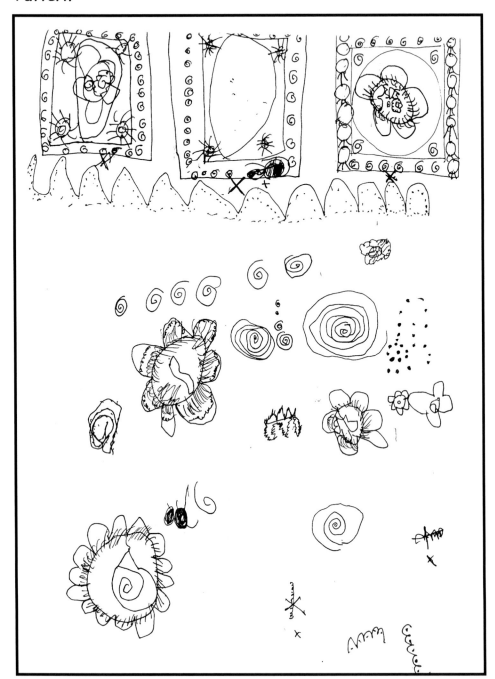

Year 2 child's drawing of patterns found on Russian artefacts

TRY THIS IDEA!

Collecting patterns from different cultures

Time	Resources	National
30–40 min.	Sketchbooks	**Curriculum**
	Pencils or fine pens	1a, 1b, 4a, 4b,
	Collection of artefacts relating to culture	4c, 5a, 5d
	being studied. Could be: fabrics, weavings,	
	pottery and carvings	
	Large piece of white paper for teacher modelling	

Introduction
'In front of us, we have this lovely collection of Indian/Russian/African things. You are going to look at them and draw some of the patterns that have been used. You are going to choose your favourite patterns and shapes and draw them in your sketchbooks.'

Practical activity
- Share out the objects.
- Choose a pattern or motif that has a repeat and draw it on a piece of paper or on the board, as an example.
- Children copy as many different patterns as they can find.
- Label them and perhaps make notes about the colours used. This could be useful if the patterns are to be used later as a starting point for printing or sewing.

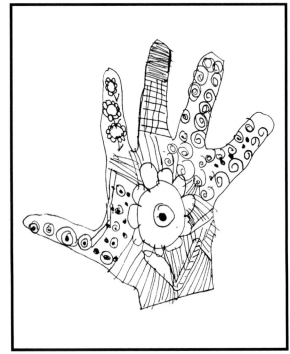

Year 2 child's drawing of Mendhi hand

Looking

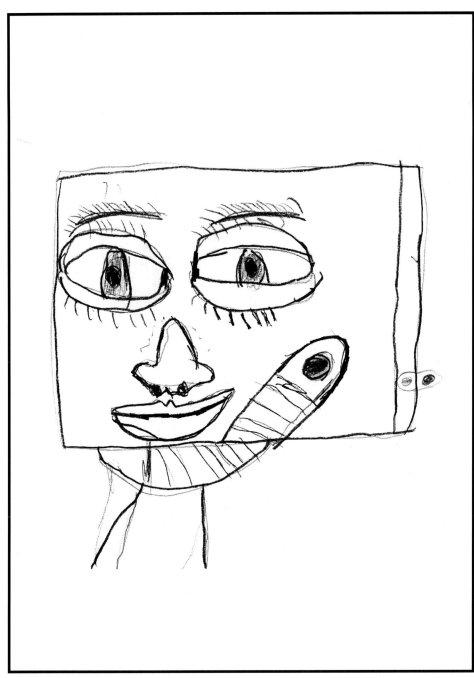

Shane Sexon, Year 2 (self-portrait done holding a mirror)

'The effort to see things without distortion takes something very like courage and this courage is essential to the artist who has to look at everything as though he saw it for the first time.'
Henri Matisse, quoted in John Elderfield, The Drawings of Henri Matisse

Introduction

Learning to draw is really a matter of learning to see. This sounds so simple. If it were simple then we would all be able to draw without needing to be taught or teach ourselves. Through learning to draw, children learn to look, and they need to look with specific intent to be able to draw well.

> 'For man's most
> noble sense is sight.'
> *Attributed to Albrecht Durer*

Why looking skills are so important

A great deal of curriculum time is given to the development of speaking and listening skills, but looking skills are overlooked. In order that drawing can be developed to the highest quality, children have to learn how to focus their whole attention on whatever it is they are drawing. Through this they will find that the longer and more concentrated the focus of attention, the more they will see.

Informed looking is very useful across the curriculum:
- ❐ In maths it develops awareness of shapes and angles, and the ability to recognize patterns
- ❐ In science it develops children's abilities to make deductions about materials
- ❐ In history children are better able to make hypotheses by looking at and handling artefacts, and by looking at historical locations and photographs
- ❐ In geography they are able to make deductions from looking at different aspects of landscapes.

The lessons in this chapter identify the different skills of looking that are essential for success in drawing.

Rationale

Learning to look carefully at the subject you are drawing is as important as, if not more important than, learning to use different media and rules about proportions. We need to help children to draw what they see, not what they think they can see. Children need help with knowing what to look for, in their subject and in their drawings, and what to do about what they see.

Happily, Key Stage 1 pupils rarely perceive drawing as a daunting task, one they either can or cannot do, as do older primary children. They are not so hooked on the idea that their drawing must 'look right'. Realism isn't so important to them. It is the confidence and animation of their drawing that is so delightful, and which we are sad to see them lose as they grow up. The drawings of young children have long inspired and fascinated adult artists.

Although Key Stage 1 children are largely engaged in narrative drawing, the seeds for looking carefully should be sown.

> 'The ability to see and the ability to draw are closely related. When we are young our seeing, drawing, reading and writing develop alongside each other, but there is an emphasis in our society on literacy and the ability to comprehend mathematical concepts. As the teaching in these subjects propels us forwards, our ability to communicate in visual terms remains underdeveloped.'
> *Ian Simpson, Drawing, Seeing and Observing*

Moving on from the schematic stage

Finding out how things really look is a gradual process helped on by investigating and recording one's impressions. At Key Stage 1 children are drawing as much by what they know as by what they see. Their drawing is often narrative and they rely on memory or schema to communicate visually.

Example of schematic figures drawn by Year 1 child

They will have developed schema with varying degrees of success. A typical schema is that of a landscape, where the sky is a horizontal blue strip at the top of the paper with a similar green one at the base to represent the ground. The sun is often a quarter circle in one upper corner of the page. There are schemas for figures, houses, trees and animals and they serve the child's purpose very well. They are as recognizable as the word 'house' or 'person' and are relatively easy to produce time and time again.

These schemas rarely overlap. Objects are drawn facing the child as if they are lined up to be seen and the most important subject matter is drawn largest.

However, there comes a time when they need to start to take another look – a careful, close, thoughtful look – and to do this most children will need guidance and encouragement.

Children's perception changes at different ages and this often relates to their maturity. The less able child will often cling to their schema because it is secure and gives them a degree of success and they know how their drawing will turn out. Abandoning schema and drawing by looking, touching and hypothesizing about the subject matter is both exciting and frightening. Suddenly drawings don't go as expected, drawing gets to be a bit of a struggle and results can be disappointing.

Children can be supported through this stage and the development of their perception encouraged in various ways. (See 'About this chapter' on page 60).

In Years 1–2 there is nothing wrong with schema; children often need to use them to create storyboards, to record ideas or to illustrate work from another curriculum area. Observational drawing can be developed alongside narrative drawing as both have their place, just as notes or plans for written work exist alongside extended writing. Teachers can introduce closer looking with younger or less able pupils through talking about, touching and describing the subject matter. This is the foundation for engaging their looking and it will feed into their drawings gradually.

About this chapter

'There is clear evidence from research in teaching young children that there is a very close connection between highly developed imaginative work and close observation.'
Roger Cole, *Drawing with Children*

In this chapter there are lessons which lay the foundations for purposeful looking:

- ❏ Children will be encouraged to look closely in a variety of ways
- ❏ They will learn to look with curiosity
- ❏ Their looking will be engaged by talking about the subjects, by questioning and hypothesizing
- ❏ They will start to collect a descriptive vocabulary
- ❏ They will have fresh vivid physical contact with the subject matter through as many senses as possible, especially through the sense of touch
- ❏ They will use focusing devices such as magnifying glasses and mirrors.

Jonathan Slacke, Year 2

List of possible subjects for drawing or discussion

Natural
Flowers
Leaves
Buds
Seeds
Seedheads
Bulbs
Sprouting beans
Grasses
Moss
Branches
Twigs
Bark
Roots
Seaweed
Shells
Dried starfish
Seahorses
Sea urchins
Crab shells
Wasps' nests
Pebbles
Fossils
Feathers
Nuts
Fruit
Vegetables
Quartz
Crystals

Man-made
Carvings
Jewellery
Embroidery
Tools
Kitchen tools
Kitchen equipment, e.g. egg
  whisks, colandars, tin
  openers, etc.
Locks
Shoes
Hats
Umbrellas
Science equipment
Pottery
Historial artefacts
Ethnic artefacts
Toys
Rope
Nets
Gardening tools
Watering cans
Brooms and brushes
Vacuum cleaners
Mops and buckets
Musical instruments
Bikes
Roller blades
Rollerskates

Workings or insides of
(broken and/or switched off!)
Clocks
Locks
Circuits
Radios
Televisions
Computers
Telephones
Engines
Engine parts
Clockwork toys
Wheels
Cogs

Animals
Alive
Minibeasts
Tadpoles
Small pets
Ants in ant colony
Worms in wormery

Dead
Stuffed animals
Stuffed birds
Stuffed fish
Mounted insects
Mounted butterflies

'For merely looking at an object
cannot be of any use to us. All looking goes
into observing, all observing into reflecting, all
reflecting into connecting, and so one can say that
with every attentive look we cast into the world
we are already theorising.'
Attributed to Johann Wolfgang von Goethe

KEY SKILL

Focusing looking through talking

Time	Resources	National
30 min.	Interesting objects that children can relate to (see list on page 61) – the more complex the subject the more scope there is for discussion Paper to collect descriptive vocabulary	Curriculum 4a

This activity can be done in relation to several other curriculum areas, such as science, history or design and technology.

Background information
The purpose of this activity is to involve the children with the subject, to help them see things they might not otherwise notice. Initially the describing could be done by the teacher to model the type of vocabulary and the range of observations possible.

These are some of the aspects of a subject that could be described:
❑ The overall shape
❑ Smaller shapes within the main outline
❑ Colours
❑ Textures
❑ Darkest and lightest areas
❑ Patterns
❑ Sounds or smells
❑ Comparative lengths and breadths
❑ Curves or angles
❑ Reflections
❑ Small details such as markings, lettering, screws, stitching
❑ The purpose or origin of the item
❑ How it was created or made, where and by whom
❑ How it looks from different angles.

When possible, children should have the opportunity to feel the items and describe the textures.

Introduction
Show the children the artefacts you have gathered to talk about. *'You are going to be looking at, touching* (if this is possible) *and talking about these objects. Let's see what your sharp artist's eyes notice.'*

Practical activity
Ask some questions to engage children's looking:
❑ What shape is it?
❑ Can you see any other shapes?
❑ Is it soft or hard?
❑ What words describe the way it feels?
❑ What colours can you see?
❑ Does it have rough/smooth/shiny/sharp/spiky/fluffy parts?
❑ What is the widest/narrowest/thickest/thinnest part of it?
❑ What is the lightest/darkest part of it?
❑ Does it look the same if I turn it over?
❑ What is this part for?
❑ How does it join on to this bit?
❑ Does it have a smell?
❑ What does the smell remind you of?
❑ How does it sound if you tap/rattle/wind/shake/drop/spin it? If you scrape a nail over it?
❑ What do you think it is made of? (Is it all made from the same material?)
❑ Is it bigger than: You? Me? This? That?
❑ Is it heavy or light?
❑ Do you think it is old or new?

USING SKILL

Talking about the subject before drawing

Time	Resources	National
45 min. approx.	Sketchbooks	Curriculum
	Drawing media appropriate to subject matter	1a, 2c, 4a, 5a
	Interesting objects that children can relate to (see list on page 61)	
	Paper to collect descriptive vocabulary	

Before starting on the practical activities, follow the pattern of focusing children's looking covered in the previous lesson. The descriptive vocabulary generated could be photocopied and stuck in their sketchbooks with the drawings. Children should have the opportunity to draw the items as soon as possible after the discussion session.

Drawing and discussion times will vary according to the complexity of the subject and the concentration levels of the children.

Practical activities

Version 1
❏ Focusing looking activity (on previous page).
❏ Draw the objects.

Version 2
❏ Draw the objects first hand or from memory (for example: *'Draw me a bicycle.'*)
❏ Focusing looking activity (on previous page).
❏ Draw objects again.
❏ Compare results, discussing any differences in the drawings. The difference in the two sets of drawings can be staggering. An even more dramatic contrast can be seen if the subject is drawn from memory first (see examples).

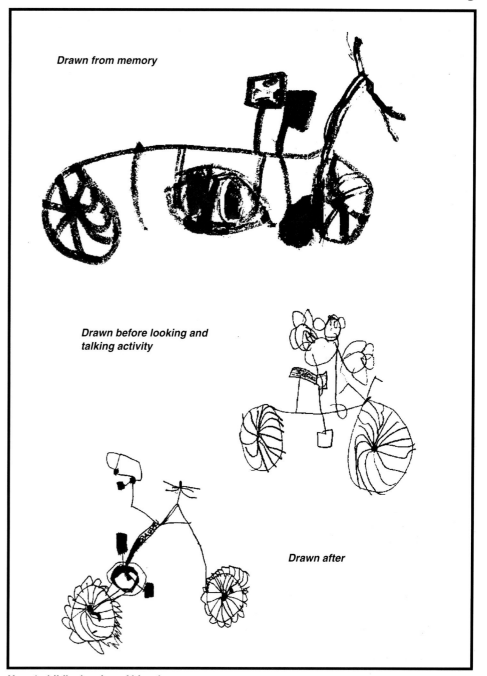

Drawn from memory

Drawn before looking and talking activity

Drawn after

Year 1 child's drawing of bicycles

SKILL

Using focusing devices

Time	Resources	National
45 min.	Magnifying glasses (as many as possible)	Curriculum
(15 min.	Plastic mirrors	1b, 4c, 5a
per	Viewfinders	
focusing	Artefacts suitable for close viewing (see list on	
device)	page 61)	
	Resource sheet 9 (page 110)	

Practical activities

The different devices can be used on different occasions. Other good works of art with lots of detail include 'National Portrait' by David Mach and 'VE Day' by LS Lowry.

'Children's Games' by Pieter Bruegel (a larger photocopiable version available on page 110).
Reproduced with permission from Kunsthistorisches Museum, Vienna

Viewfinders

❏ The children should place the viewfinders over an area of the picture and then discuss, report or record what they see.

❏ They can slide the viewfinder around and select different areas to investigate.

❏ This could be done with pictures connected to topics being studied, such as buildings. Children could look at enlarged photographs of streets and find different tiles, doors, windows or brick patterns.

Mirrors

❏ Children could look first at their eyes, inside their mouths, etc.

❏ They should then look at a friend's reflection, noting the differences between their usual view of their friend and the reflected view.

❏ Children can stand the mirror next to an object and look at its reflection, altering the angle and noting the changes.

Magnifying glasses

❏ Magnifying glasses are excellent for investigating the natural world.

❏ Children could share items and discuss what they see that they didn't see so well without the lenses.

❏ Descriptive vocabulary could be collected.

Background information

Viewfinders are very useful for focusing children's looking on areas of a complex picture, in order to research subject matter or techniques used. They isolate areas of a subject and cut out other visual information that might confuse or distract children. Viewfinders can be made from stiff card. Black is best as it does not distract the eye from the subject. Cut an aperture (square, rectangular or even a keyhole shape) in the middle of the card.

Magnifying glasses can be used in two ways: to look closely at the object before and while drawing the whole thing, or to draw different parts of one object. They help children to notice fine detail.

Mirrors are a useful way to look at things from unusual angles and for self-portraits. They can be used in different ways to enhance children's looking.

USING SKILL

Using magnifying glasses

Time	Resources	National
30–40 min.	Magnifying glasses, one per child Sketchbooks Drawing pencils or fine line pens Artefacts to draw (topic-related or see list on page 61)	**Curriculum** 1a, 2c, 4a, 5a

Introduction
'Today you are going to draw (whatever). *First we are going to talk about what you can see, and then you will draw* (the object) *using the magnifying glasses to help you to see all sorts of little details that perhaps you didn't notice before.'*

Practical activity
❏ Spend a few minutes engaging children's looking by talking about shapes, textures, etc. (see Focusing looking activity on page 62).
❏ Encourage children to say what they can see and feel.
❏ Children draw the whole artefact, naming it.
❏ They draw a more detailed study of different parts.
❏ They could be encouraged to look at how one part joins onto or grows out of another and how the textures or patterns change from one area to another.
❏ They could record and label several different parts of an object, for example with a plant drawing: buds, leaves, sepals, petals, stalks, seedheads, seeds, patterns on petals, holes or marks made by insects, colour changes, etc.

Background information
Viewfinders and mirrors are excellent focusing devices, but magnifying glasses are probably the most useful device to use in drawing, particularly when drawing and researching from the natural world. It can be a good idea to allow the children to use the magnifying glasses to look at whatever catches their fancy for a few minutes at the beginning of the lesson. They will doubtless look up each other's noses, etc., but it is better they get this out of their systems at the outset, in the hope they won't do it during the lesson!

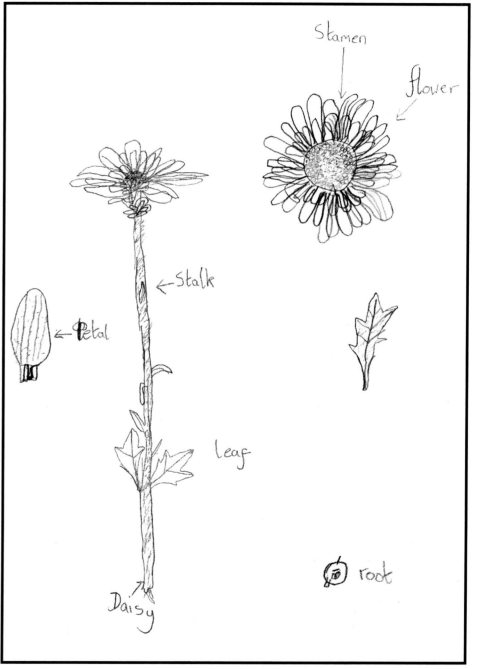

Archie Muirhead, Year 2 (drawing of flower and parts of a flower using a magnifying glass)

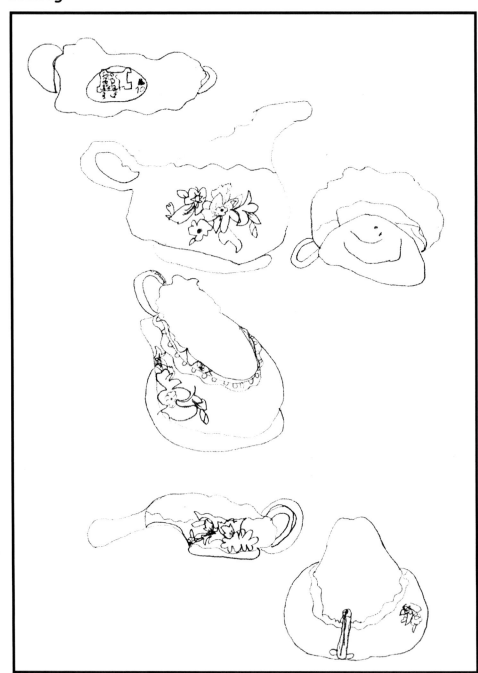

Chloe Gregory, Year 2 (drawing of a jug from different viewpoints)

 TRY THIS IDEA!

Looking and drawing from different viewpoints

Time	Resources	National
20 min.	Sketchbooks	**Curriculum**
	B or 2B pencils	1a, 4a
	Cups, mugs, teapots, jugs, plastic animals or figures (or any artefacts that look different from different angles) (see list on page 61)	

Introduction
'Today you are going to be drawing objects from different views. You can draw the different views on the same page. Your drawings will show what the object looks like all over, not just from one side.'

Practical activity
- Hold up an item and demonstrate to the children how it looks from one particular view.
- Ask them to tell you what they can see of it.
- Then change the view. Point out the parts that are now out of view and parts that can now be seen.
- Repeat this with as many different viewpoints as possible.
- Tell the children to arrange their object in a view they like and to draw exactly what they can see.
- Then suggest they change the view and draw that. Allow about four or five minutes for each drawing.
- Point out that they can draw the object from above, and upside down, from both sides and any other views they can find.

Background information
It can help children to draw what they do see, rather than what they think they can see, if they draw an object from different views. The different views can be done on the same sheet of paper. Encourage children to label the drawings: above, underneath, left side, etc.

William Taylor-Jones, Year 2

Figures and faces

Rationale

One of the most important aspects of school life is the adults and children who make up the school community. Therefore what could be more useful or relevant to children in drawing than to be able to draw people?

Drawing people (figure drawing) is a fundamental part of art education. Children are quite likely to be asked to include people in illustrations across the curriculum. That probably means being able to do it from memory. They need to be able to draw figures with fairly accurate proportions, quickly and easily. To do this they need to be taught a few basic rules, and they need practice.

Drawing people is like drawing anything else in so much as you need to look hard at the subject. However, it is more obvious when the drawing doesn't go well, since we all know what people look like.

In this chapter children will learn some of the basic rules of figure drawing. Both year groups will draw from life and from memory. They will study both head, and whole-body portraits. They will evaluate their drawings and identify what they might change in their work.

Depicting the human form is the drawing skill that children will use most in primary school.

Common pitfalls

There are some inaccuracies that crop up almost universally when children draw faces and figures:

- ❏ Heads tend to be too big
- ❏ Eyes are too near the top of the head
- ❏ Necks are missing
- ❏ Shoulders are too narrow
- ❏ Arms are too short and with younger children they stick straight out to the sides
- ❏ Feet are too small
- ❏ Both feet point the same way, or
- ❏ Feet are at a 180-degree angle to each other.

In this chapter children will be given strategies to deal with these tendencies, and some tips to make it easier to put things right for themselves.

Example of common pitfalls

Shapes and proportions

Here are some simple pointers about average body proportions and shapes. Children won't always remember these guidelines but they are a useful foundation for Key Stage 2. They are intended only as a starting point, not as a formula. Photocopiable versions of these pointers appear on Resource sheets 10 and 11 (see pages 111 and 112).

Figure drawing

- ❐ Heads are a lot smaller than bodies.
- ❐ Head and body shapes are more oval than round.
- ❐ Arms and legs have a thickness (not single lines).
- ❐ Feet are flatish ovals.
- ❐ You can fit about 5–6 heads into a child's body (6–7 into an adult's body).
- ❐ The middle of the body is the hip line (not the waist).
- ❐ Arms (when hanging down) end half way down the thighs.
- ❐ Shoulders are at least twice the width of the face.

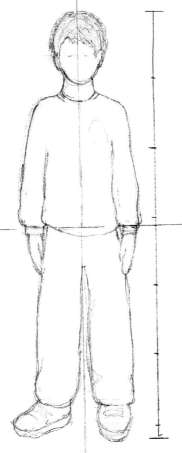

$\frac{1}{2}$

Facial portraits

- ❐ Heads are more oval than round.
- ❐ Eyes are almond shaped.
- ❐ Eyes come about half way down the face.
- ❐ You can rarely see the whole iris.
- ❐ Mouths have two lips.
- ❐ Hairline starts below the top of the head (unless model is balding!).
- ❐ *Useful reminder:* EVERYONE has a neck!

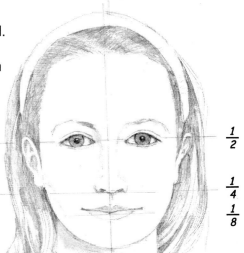

$\frac{1}{2}$

$\frac{1}{4}$
$\frac{1}{8}$

About this chapter

When children have passed the 'head legger' stage of figure drawing and are drawing recognizable people, they are probably ready to learn how they can improve their figure and face drawing.

When children are involved in narrative drawing it is not relevant to comment on drawing inaccuracies, as the story is the focus not the drawing. However, when they are doing a lesson on portraits, it is a good time to explain some rules about face and body proportions.

In this chapter children will study and draw faces. They will use Plasticine and collage to help support their awareness of the position of facial features.

They will draw figures from life and from memory. Their attention will be drawn to common misconceptions about face and body proportions.

They will evaluate their drawings and identify what they might change in future work.

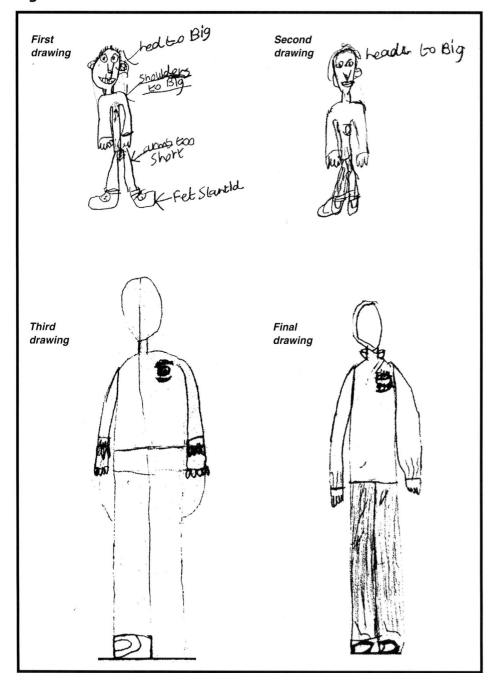

First drawing

Second drawing

Third drawing

Final drawing

Thomas Ellis, Year 2 (drawings done at same session, with child's own evaluations)

KEY SKILL

Drawing the whole body 1

Time:	Resources	National
30–40 min.	Sketchbooks	Curriculum
	B pencil	1a, 1b, 3a, 3b,
	Resource sheet 10 (see page 111)	5a

The teacher could be the model, that way no child misses this initial session. It is quite useful to be able to watch them drawing and note how often they look at you. It should be 50% looking and 50% drawing. This lesson needs to be done quite often. Their figure drawing skills will improve greatly with practice.

Introduction
'You are going to be learning how to get better at drawing people.'

Practical activity
❏ Read/show the figure guidelines (Resource sheet 10).
❏ Tell children to use light lines.
❏ Allow 7–10 minutes to draw the whole figure.
❏ Stress the children should draw the whole figure from head to feet, leaving out facial features, patterns on clothes, etc. and concentrate on body shapes and proportions.
❏ When they have drawn the whole figure, ask them to look at their drawings and check the guidelines outlined at the start of the lesson.
❏ They could mark their drawings in some way to indicate how well they think they have succeeded.
❏ Ask them to think about how they will improve in their next drawing.
❏ Repeat the activity as often as you have time for.

Background information
There are two vital points that need to be made to children at the beginning. Firstly, do not draw any detail: no eyes, nose, mouth, no patterns on clothes. If they draw detail they do not focus on getting the whole figure drawn. Secondly, draw with very light lines. Explain that they may well want to change something, and if they have drawn dark lines it will be very hard to make changes. See notes on light lines, page 16.

KEY SKILL Drawing the whole body 2

Time	Resources	National
40 min.	Sketchbooks	**Curriculum**
	B pencil	1a, 2b, 3a, 3b,
	Resource sheet 10 (see page 111)	5a

Introduction
'You have been drawing the whole body and trying to get the shapes right. Now you are getting better at that, you can spend a little longer on each drawing.'

Practical activity
❏ Set up a simple standing pose, arms relaxed by sides.
❏ Remind the children of the body proportions.
❏ The children do a quick light drawing of the whole figure.
❏ Introduce the information that about five or six heads fit into the length of a child's body (six or seven in an adult). Show them how to measure the head they have drawn, with their fingers, and check how many will fit into the body.
❏ Explain that if they can fit in fewer than five or six heads they must have drawn the head too big and they should adjust the size in their drawing.
❏ Next talk about details. Draw their attention to clothes, tones and patterns. At this stage they can also add features.
❏ Allow time at the end of each pose, for the children to consider their success against the pointers they were given, and to consider what they will improve.
❏ Repeat the activity.
❏ Year 2 children could gradually increase the length of time for each pose.

Background information
Once children are able to draw the whole figure with reasonable shapes and proportions, they can spend longer on the pose, adding details and tone. If the models are children, allow them a two-minute break every five minutes. This time can be used by the other children to check their shapes and proportions, and consider their next steps.

Daisy Barker, Year 2

Figures and faces

Year 1 child's drawing of a parent
wearing his life boatman uniform

Thomas Ellis, Year 1 (pastel drawing
of classmate wearing a ballet dress)

Drawing poses in costume

Time	Resources	National Curriculum
40 min.	Sketchbooks	1a, 1b, 3a, 3b, 5a
	Any drawing media (charcoal is good for quick sketches, 2B or B pencils for more detailed studies	
	Resource sheet 10 (see page 111)	
	Models in costumes, see note below	

To add variety to figure drawing, it is useful to give the children the stimulus of drawing different models in different outfits.

Adults who might be persuaded to pose:
❏ Parents who have uniforms or other work-related clothing: nurses, police, cooks and builders
❏ Adults working in the school: caretaker, dinner staff, classroom support staff
❏ Parents who have special clothing for leisure activities: dancing, sports, amateur dramatics
❏ People in the community who have national or traditional costumes.

Children could pose in:
❏ Bridesmaid or pageboy outfits
❏ Sports kits
❏ Show costumes
❏ National costumes or outfits borrowed from role play or dressing-up box
❏ Costumes linked to topics: people who help us, clothes in the past, etc.

Practical activity

❏ Set up a standing pose – it will be easier for the children to check body proportions. Remind them of the basic rules of these. Draw attention to position of arms, legs, feet, etc.

❏ Suggest they draw the whole figure lightly first, starting with the head (leaving out facial features and details).

❏ Remind them to check how many heads they can fit into the body and make it bigger or smaller if necessary at this stage, not wait until the drawing is nearly finished. (This is a good time for the model to have a short break.)

❏ Once they are satisfied they have got the main proportions as accurately as they can, suggest that now they add facial features, clothing detail and some tones, patterns and textures.

❏ Use the model's breaks for evaluation: ask the children to think about how they will improve and develop their drawings next.

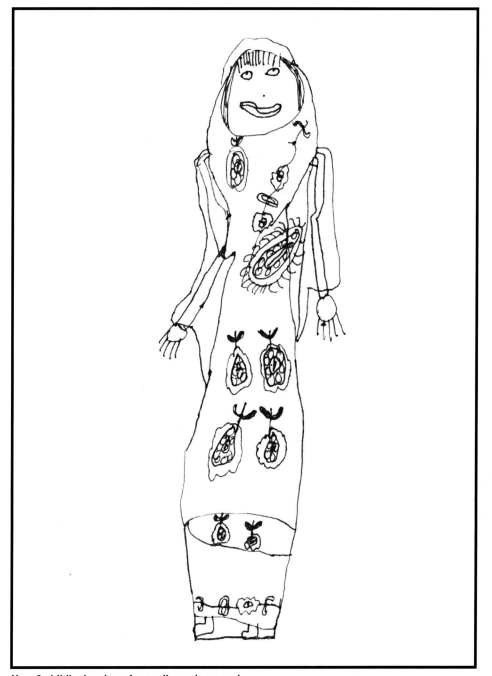

Year 2 child's drawing of a pupil wearing a sari

Year 2 child's pastel portait showing face divisions to position features

 SKILL

Drawing heads and position of features 1

Time	Resources	National
30 min.	Sketchbooks	Curriculum
	B or 2B pencils	4a
	or chalky pastels on mid-tone sugar paper	
	Resource sheet 11 (see page 112)	

Introduction

'Today you are going to be getting better at drawing faces. You often need to draw people so it is very useful to be able to do it well.'

Practical activity

❏ Talk about head shape first. Explain that although head and face shapes vary from person to person, they are mostly oval. You could say, 'Think rugby ball, not football.'

❏ Draw a large oval on the board.

❏ Ask the children to draw a large oval lightly in their sketchbooks. Some will need support with this.

❏ Ask the children where they think the eyes come, then explain that, in fact, they come half-way down the face. They generally find this hard to believe, so ask a child to come to the front, and measure the eye position. Suggest that they walk their fingers up and down their faces to check for themselves.

❏ On the board, draw a horizontal line half way across the oval and a vertical line, dividing the oval in half.

❏ Get the children do the same. Then get them to draw in eyes on the horizontal line, leaving a space between them. They should then put in eyebrows above.

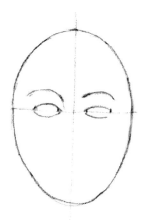

❏ On the board again, draw a line half way between the eyes and the chin. Explain that this is roughly where the nose ends. Draw their attention to the shape of the nostrils.

❏ Children draw the bottom of the nose along that line.

❏ Now draw the mouth half way between the nostrils and the chin.

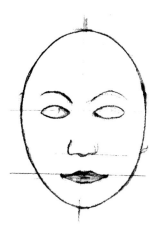

❏ Lastly, add the ears (tops in line with eyebrows), hair and neck, which should start below the ears.

Background information
Children tend to draw eyes too near the top of the head. This could be because they consider the eyes to be the most important facial feature. Whatever the reason, it is a hard habit to change.

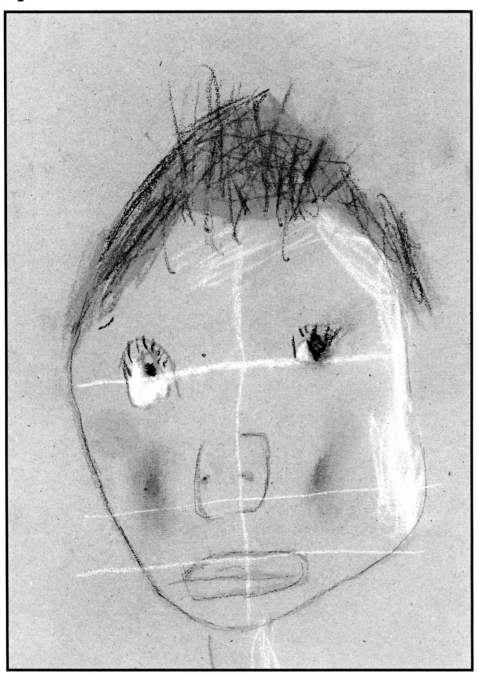

Year 1 child's pastel drawing using facial divisions

 Drawing heads and position of features 2

Time	Resources	National
30 min.	Sketchbooks or A4 paper	Curriculum
	B or 2B pencils or felt tips	1a, 3a, 3b
	or chalky pastels on mid-tone sugar paper	
	Resource sheet 11 (see page 112)	

Introduction
'You have been finding out what shape heads are and where the eyes, nose and mouth come on the face. Now you are going to draw a person from your imagination or memory and see if you can get all the features in the right place.'

Practical activity
❐ Children draw an oval for the head first. Less able and younger children will need help with this.
❐ Indicate with their fingers on the face to show the position for the eyes, then draw a line across where the eyes will be and a line down to indicate the centre. Year 2 children could divide the lower half of the face in half again to indicate where the base of the nose will go.
❐ Next draw in the features in this order: eyes, bottom of nose, mouth, eyebrows, and ears (if in view).
❐ Before the children draw in the hair, talk to them about where the hairline starts; draw their attention to the fact that it does not start on the top of the head.
❐ Use a few children with different hairstyles as models.
❐ Note how far down the face some fringes come.
❐ Children could evaluate their drawings against Resource sheet 11, and then decide what they could change or improve on next time.
❐ They could say why they are pleased/not pleased with their work and whose drawings they think are good and why.

Background information
It does not really matter what medium is used for this activity. The focus of the lesson is the shape of the head and position of features. If pencil or pastels are used then children have the added advantage that they can use light lines and add tone. Felt tips can create quite a pleasing piece of final artwork which could be displayed.

This is not really a picture of anyone in particular, but rather an opportunity to create a face or reproduce one from memory, using the general rules of portraits.

Year 1 children and less able Year 2 children might need to have an oval shape lightly drawn for them. The scale of the head, as well as the shape, can be rather challenging.

Sarah Vanstone, Year 2 (felt tip drawing of a face)

Coralie Thomson, Year 1

 USING SKILL

Position of features 1

Time	Resources	National
30–40 min.	Large pictures of faces from magazines (at least one per child); could be photocopies	**Curriculum** 1a, 2a, 5c
	A4 paper or sketchbooks	
	Any pencil	
	Scissors	
	Glue sticks	

Introduction

'You have been working hard to remember what shape people's heads are and where the features are on their faces. Today you are going to create a face using eyes, noses, mouths, eyebrows and ears cut from magazines.'

Practical activity

☐ Children cut out all the main features from a photograph of a face (cut out complete eyes including lashes).

☐ Next they draw an oval for the head that they think will be about right for the size of features they have. Younger pupils will need help with this.

☐ Children arrange the features where they think they should go. This is a good opportunity to explain that if they move the features around a little they can create very different characters: eyes close together, longer space between nose and top lip, etc.

☐ When the features are arranged reasonably accurately, they can be stuck down.

☐ Hair can be drawn or stuck on.

☐ The finished faces can be cut out and stuck down on unusual backgrounds, such as bricks or sky; this creates a rather surrealist effect.

Background information

This activity can be very useful for reinforcing the knowledge of head shape and position of features.

Position of features 2

Time	Resources	National
40 min. (longer if using clay)	A4 (approx) thin card Plasticine or clay If clay is used – rolling pins, clay tools, boards, pieces of sacking to place under work	**Curriculum** 1a, 2a, 5c

Introduction
'You have been working hard to remember what shape people's heads are and where the features are on their faces. Today you are going to create a face using Plasticine (or clay).'

Practical activities

Plasticine
☐ Children roll a long thin snake of Plasticine in their hands, and then lay it on the card in an oval shape.
☐ They make eyeballs and position them correctly on the face. Year 2 children could make thin strips to be placed as the outline of eyelids.
☐ Repeat this with nose, mouth, eyebrows, ears and hair.

Clay
☐ Children roll out a piece of clay and cut it into an oval. (Some children will need support with this.)
☐ They make eyeballs and position them correctly on the face. More able children could make thin strips to be placed as the outline of eyelids.
☐ Fix all features with a little very wet clay as glue, and by making small score marks beneath textures.
☐ Repeat this with the nose, mouth, eyebrows, ears and hair.
☐ Texture can be added with clay tools: freckles, beard hair.

Background information
This activity can be very useful to reinforce the knowledge of head shape and position of features.

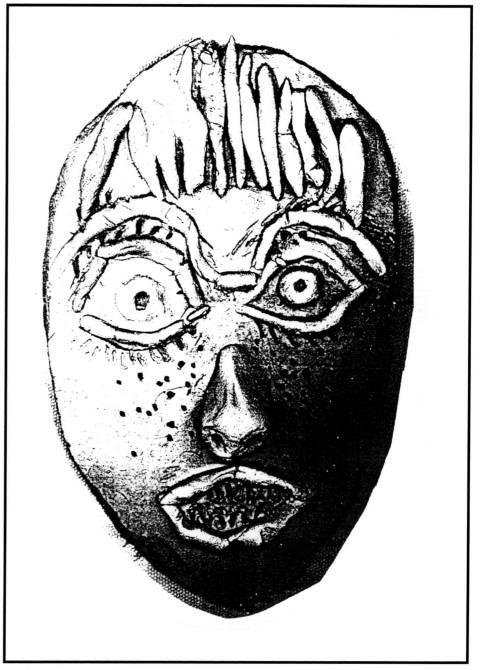

Archie Muirhead, Year 2 (clay head)

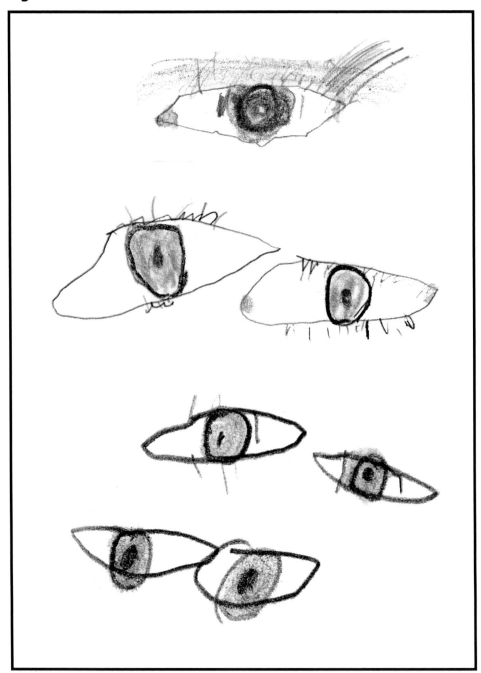

Year 1 children's attempts at drawing eyes elongated rather than round

 SKILL

Drawing eyes and mouths

Time	Resources	National
45 min. approx.	Sketchbooks B or 2B pencils Mirrors (plastic)	**Curriculum** 1a, 1b, 2b, 5a

Introduction
'You have been learning about where eyes and mouths are on a face and getting better at drawing them in the right positions. Now you are going to spend more time drawing just eyes and mouths.'

Practical activity
❑ Children draw a pair of eyes and a mouth. Most of them will probably draw the eyes: completely round, or with the whole iris showing, or with eyelashes like railings all round the eye, and without pupils or eyelids. The mouths will probably have a single lip.
❑ Now ask them to look in the mirror and talk about the shape of their eyes. They might come up with shape names like 'a lemon', 'a boat' or 'an almond'.
❑ Draw attention to the fact that you cannot see the whole of the iris. The top and the bottom are generally hidden by the eyelids.
❑ Ask them to look at where their eyelashes grow from, and the angle from the lid (to the side rather than upwards).
❑ Next concentrate on the pupil and how much darker it is than the iris. Point out the dot of reflected light near the middle.
❑ Children now draw their own eyes, remembering to include all the things they have just been looking at.

- ❏ Repeat this activity with mouths. Point out that they have an upper and lower lip. You could say they are rather like two worms, and like worms they have little lines on them.
- ❏ Ask them to draw sad mouths, angry, frightened, shouting mouths. Look at open mouths: how many teeth can be seen?
- ❏ They might like to label their drawings, e.g. 'a mouth singing', 'a crying mouth'.

Background information
Most children have developed schema for drawing eyes and mouths. Eyes are drawn round and mouths as a single curved line. This lesson encourages them to have another look at the shapes and draw what they see rather than what they think they know about them. Noses are actually quite difficult, so children could just draw the nostril shapes.

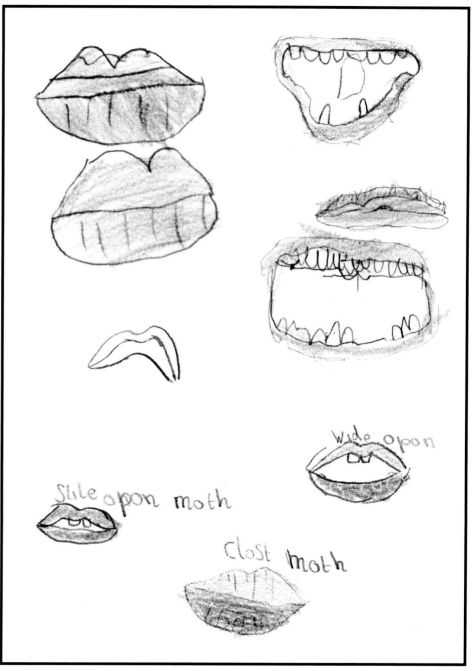

Year 2 children's drawings of mouths showing upper and lower lips, open or closed

Archie Muirhead, Year 2

 USING SKILL

Face portraits

Time	Resources	National
30 min.	Sketchbooks	**Curriculum**
	B pencils	1a, 1b, 2b, 5a
	If you have them, people crayons (see Glossary), if not, pencil alone is fine	
	Mirrors if they are doing self-portraits	

Introduction

'Today you are going to draw portraits. You are going to draw just faces, not the whole body. I will be looking to see if you have remembered all the things you learned about head shapes, what the eyes, nose and mouth really look like, and where they come on the face.'

Practical activity

❐ Revise the aspects of portraits covered so far: the oval head shape, the position and shape of features. (Children could be drawing themselves or each other.)

❐ They should start by lightly drawing an oval shape for the head. Stress that this should fill the paper so they will have plenty of room to draw the features. Younger or less able children will need help with this.

❐ They draw the neck, noting how wide it is.

❐ Now they divide the oval into quarters with one light horizontal and one light vertical line. Model this on the board.

❐ They draw a further horizontal line to divide the lower half equally. Model. Younger and less able children will need help. They now have a basic frame on which to place the features.

❐ Remind them to look carefully before drawing the eyes and mouth, and to remember what they have learned about their shapes.

❐ Draw their attention to the eyebrows and the shape and position of the nose. They could include the hollow above the top lip and any shadows they can see.

❐ Before they add the hair, tell them to look carefully to see where it grows from, how far down the face it comes, if it covers the neck, whether it is wavy or straight, and if the ears are visible.

❐ Lastly they could add details, freckles, moles, etc., and some tone or colour.

Chalk and charcoal

Year 1 child's charcoal and chalk cube (cube outline drawn by adult)

Year 1 child's artwork (mixed-media collage, including pen, chalk and pastel – see colour example on front cover)

Rationale

Chalk and charcoal are excellent drawing media as they encourage children to think about a whole subject and not to become lost in detail, as they often do. For example, they will carefully draw eyelashes when they have not yet drawn the whole figure, they will start to draw patterns on clothing before they have checked body proportions.

Chalk and charcoal encourage them to think big, to concentrate on main features and to think about lights and darks from the moment they put their first marks on paper.

Drawing with chalk and charcoal will help children to get into the habit of seeing and thinking in tones, rather than detail and colour. It can be free, messy and dramatic, or controlled, delicate and subtle. It is also relatively easy to create pleasing pictures and so helps to boost confidence and self-esteem.

Nicky Loat, Year 1 (Houses of Parliament)

Chalk and charcoal are classic drawing media. Across the ages artists have used these drawing materials, for example Rembrandt, Whistler and the contemporary American artist Jim Dine.

Media knowledge

Charcoal is made by sophisticated methods nowadays, but it is basically just burned wood and is the oldest drawing medium. It has been in use since early cave people covered the walls of their caves with drawings of the animals they hunted, using burned sticks from their fires and charred bones. It has been made for centuries by the controlled and partial burning of wood. It makes bold black marks, which can be smudged, blended and lightened in different ways.

Chalk is often used with charcoal as a way of picking out highlights and for mixing with charcoal to create mid tones. Adding chalk highlights can bring a charcoal drawing to life, giving it contrast and sparkle.

Different types of charcoal
Stick charcoal
The commonest types of charcoal are vine and willow charcoal, which are made in different thicknesses and with different degrees of hardness. Medium thickness is the most versatile, although the fine is useful for more delicate work and the thick for drawings covering large areas or dense coverage. Children tend to worry about charcoal breaking so it is a good idea to snap it into approximately 4 cm lengths in advance.

Charcoal pencils
These are a less messy way of using charcoal as the children's fingers hold the wooden shaft not the actual charcoal, and broken pieces are not forever dropping on the floor. However, they need constant sharpening, so can be more trouble than they are worth.

Compressed charcoal
These small sticks are made from powdered charcoal compressed with a binding material. They do not break as easily as stick charcoal but they are less easy to dust off.

Chalk
Ordinary blackboard chalk is perfectly adequate. White chalk pastels or Conté crayons (soft pastels) could also be used.

Fixing drawings
All soft media like chalk and charcoal need 'fixing' as these materials are so soft they will continue to smudge and fade if not fixed when the drawing is finished. Special fixative can be purchased from art suppliers but cheap unscented hairspray makes an acceptable alternative. The drawings should be sprayed when children are out of the room.

Joe Blackford, Year 1 (chalk and charcoal drawing of 1950s black telephone)

Tips and techniques

To avoid smudging during drawing
One of the characteristics of chalk and charcoal is that they smudge.
Drawings can be spoiled by being leaned on as work progresses so
provide the children with pieces of scrap paper to lay between their hands
and the drawing. Their hands will rest on this and not on their drawing.

Papers
Chalk and charcoal work looks best on mid-tone tinted sugar paper such
as grey, buff or brown. Charcoal is sympathetic to the texture of paper
allowing the grain to show through, so paper with a slight roughness to it
is ideal. Very smooth or shiny paper should be avoided as the charcoal
will slide on the surface and lose its density.

Blending
To create an expanse of blended tone, first build up an area of scribbled
marks, pressing evenly but not too heavily. Use the tip of a finger to rub
the surface lightly to blend the marks together. The finished effect is a soft
deep shadow which can be drawn over or made deeper by repeating the
process. Chalk and charcoal can be blended in the same way.

Lightening
Charcoal can be lifted or lightened in different ways: a soft eraser, pieces
of cloth, tissues or even pellets of soft bread. If erasers are being used
they need to be as soft as possible, and kept just for use with charcoal, as
cleaning them after will take time. Some old erasers could be cut into
quarters, as children do not need a whole eraser each.

Charcoal wash
A brush dipped in water applied to parts or the whole of a charcoal
drawing creates a grey wash. The tones of the wash soften the fierceness
of the black lines and when the wash is dry it can be drawn over, creating
a layered effect.

Keeping clean
Children should cover their clothes and roll up or push back their sleeves.
They can become agitated at the state of their hands during a charcoal
lesson. Explain that some aspects of art are messy and that's just the way
it is. Discourage washing hands during the lesson; they should just dust
their hands together to get the worst off, and carry on.

Photocopying
Chalk and charcoal drawings can be photocopied and then colour added.
This can be very effective (see mixed-media collage on page 83 and on
front cover).

About this chapter

It is quite easy for children to create dramatic and pleasing effects using
chalk and charcoal.

They are ideal media for capturing spectacular scenes, for example a
sudden fall of snow, or a stormy sky and lashing rain.

Chalk and charcoal can also be used to great effect in portrait work; the
chalk highlights 'lift' the drawings, giving them a sparkle and crispness.
Children are often delighted with the results.

In this chapter children will experiment with making marks with chalk and
charcoal. They will blend and smudge them together and use chalk to
create simple highlights. Then they will use these skills to create a
drawing using both media.

Thomas Corras, Year 1 (the Great Fire of London)

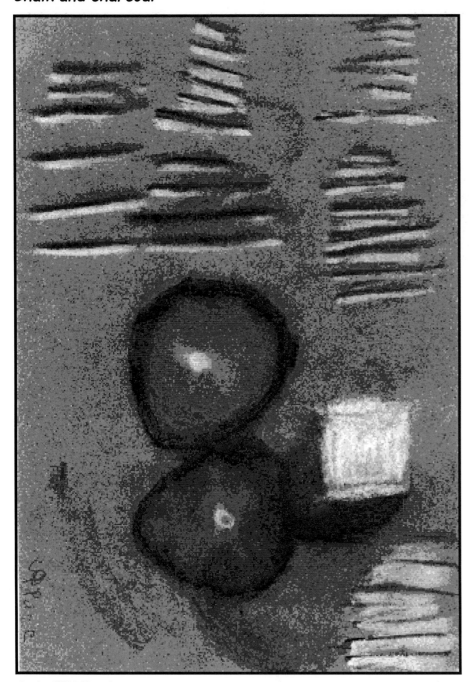

Jordan Wild, Year 1

 KEY SKILL

Making and blending marks in chalk and charcoal

Time	Resources	National
15 min.	Mid-tone sugar paper	Curriculum
	Medium charcoal pieces, approx. 4 cm long	2a, 4a
	White chalk	
	Aprons or painting shirts	
	Fixative (see page 85 and Glossary)	

Introduction

'Lots of artists use chalk and charcoal to draw with. Charcoal makes lovely dark marks and the chalk looks very white and bright next to it. Artists call this "contrast". Another lovely thing about charcoal is the fact it smudges. If you smudge chalk and charcoal together they make a grey colour – this is called blending.'

Practical activity

❏ Tell the children to make some lines with chalk, and to smudge some of them.

❏ Next they draw some lines in charcoal next to the chalk lines and smudge some of these together.

❏ They can experiment drawing patches of chalk and charcoal and blending them to see what different tones of grey they can make.

❏ Tell them to draw a circle and a square in chalk and leave them empty.

❏ Now challenge them to make light grey circles and squares and dark grey circles and squares in another space.

❏ While they are doing this, go round the class and turn their squares into cubes (see page 39).

- ❏ Next tell them to shade one side of their cube a medium grey, one side all black charcoal and one side with white chalk. They should be able to see how this makes the cube look more solid.
- ❏ Lastly they could run their fingers round the inside edge of the circle darkening it and then add a small chalk highlight in the middle. Their circle should now be transformed into a sphere.

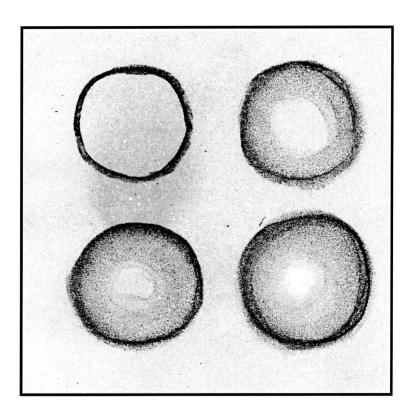

Background information
This activity helps children understand the character and possibilities of chalk and charcoal. It is an opportunity for them to experiment with and investigate the media before they embark on a drawing, as charcoal is not an easy medium to control. There are two charcoal activities in the Tone chapter on pages 41–42.

Victoria Rawlings, Year 2

Year 1 child's drawing of 1950s black telephone

*George Porter,
Year 1*

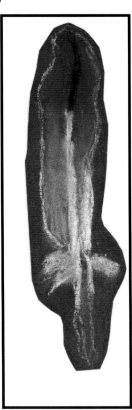

*Year 2 child's
chalk drawing of
feather*

USING SKILL

Drawing with chalk and charcoal

Time	Resources	National Curriculum
30–40 min.	Mid-tone sugar paper Medium thickness charcoal pieces, approx. 4 cm long White chalk Aprons or painting shirts Fixative (see page 85 and Glossary) Artefacts that are mostly black with some lighter areas, e.g. umbrella, old telephone, tape recorder, radio, Wellington boots, PE shoes	1a, 2b, 4a

Introduction

'You have been experimenting with making marks and blending chalk and charcoal. Now you are going to use chalk and charcoal to do some drawings.'

Practical activity 1

☐ Put out one artefact per group of children.

☐ Children lightly outline the shape of it in white chalk.

☐ They should draw and shade in the lightest area they can see in chalk.

☐ Next look at the darkest areas and draw those in with the charcoal.

☐ If they can see any areas that are grey they should shade those in lightly in charcoal scribbles then some chalk scribbles and blend the two with their fingers.

☐ The artefacts could be swapped around so everyone has the opportunity to draw a different subject.

Practical activity 2

❏ Chalk and charcoal are excellent for figure drawing.

❏ Children lightly draw the whole figure first in chalk.

❏ Next they should stop drawing and look at the figure to decide which areas are dark, which mid tone and which light.

❏ They could shade in the darkest areas first; they may need some discussion to help them spot these.

❏ Now add the lightest details in white chalk. Year 2 children and more able Year 1 children could attempt to blend mid-tone areas they have noticed.

Jordan

Jordan Wild, Year 1 (Mona Lisa drawn on mid-tone paper, see colour version on front cover)

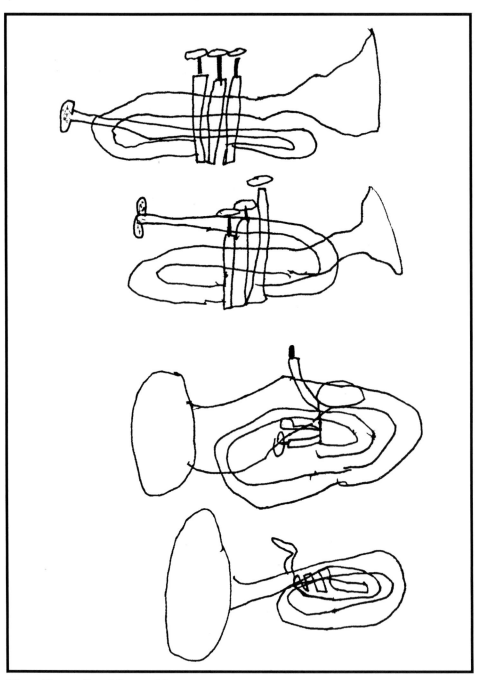

Ebony Thorne, Year 2 (trumpets)

Evaluation and assessment

Assessment

Children need to reflect on their artwork and should share in assessment where appropriate. They should be clear which aspect of their artwork is being assessed, and what they need to do to meet the assessment criteria.

Realistically, drawing needs only to be assessed in broad terms: identify those children who are struggling and will need to cover the work again or in a different way, and those children who have excelled and could be stretched.

One way might be to broadly group pupils into three ability bands. At the end of a term, chapter or whenever appropriate, select a small number of pupils from each band and assess their work. From this make a general assumption that other pupils in the same band will have achieved a similar standard. At the end of the next term or chapter, select a different group of pupils so that over the course of a term (or a year) all pupils will have been assessed.

Another way to make the assessment process easier is to photocopy the class list and attach it to the drawing skills assessment sheet (Resource sheet 12, page 113). Highlight the aspect(s) you are going to assess. (Limit this to a maximum of three, unless this is an end of year assessment.) Then, using a colour code (e.g. green for excellent, yellow for satisfactory and red for problems), highlight the children's names with the appropriate colours on the class list. Further comments could be added if necessary. This could be shortened to highlighting those achieving well above and well below.

Drawing assessments

Class:

Date:

Colour code
Green = Excellent
Yellow = Satisfactory
Red = Needs further help

1. Uses a variety of lines in drawings
2. Uses tone in drawings
3. Identifies areas for development in own drawings

	1	2	3
John Brown			
Priya Gil			
Mary Green			
An Other			

Example of assessment record

Evaluation and assessment

Assessment should inform planning. If the majority of the class have not met the success criteria, the task needs to be re-evaluated.

Try to be specific when making your judgements:
- ☐ Was it too hard?
- ☐ Was the explanation clear enough?
- ☐ Does it need to be done again in the same way or differently?
- ☐ Which elements of my teaching do I need to change?
- ☐ When and how will this be done in the same way or differently?

Figure and face drawings could be assessed against the shapes and proportions guidelines found on page 69 and Resource sheets 10 and 11 (pages 111 and 112).

Older or more able children could check their own drawings, write comments on their achievements and give themselves targets, as in this example:

> *'I am pleased with my figure drawing, it turned out well and I remembered to draw in the neck which I used to forget. I want to get better at drawing shoulders. I always draw them too small.'*
>
> Megan, age 7

It is as well to model self-evaluation and targets on the board or the children may set themselves unrealistically hard targets and say something like: *'I want to get better at drawing ponies.'* There is further information about self-evaluation on pages 95–96.

Using success criteria to evaluate children's work

Success criteria should really be drawn up with the pupils as the direct teaching or explanation is taking place. For example, after the skill has been taught but before it is going to be used in a context, say, *'We have been learning how to make our drawings more interesting by using lots of different lines. I want you to remember to use as many of the different kinds of lines as you think will be right for the job in your drawings today* (run over the variety of lines covered). *I shall be looking at your drawings to see if you have used a range of lines.'*

Use a 'must, should, could' system of success criteria. For example, for a Year 1–2 lesson on line work in pencil, write up on the board:

> **Success criteria**
> 1. You **must** use lots of different lines.
> 2. You **should** try to use both dark lines and light lines.
> 3. You **could** use both the side and the point of the pencil.

Work can then be judged against these criteria. Three criteria are the maximum for Key Stage 1.

Success criteria are also useful for children's self-assessment.

There are success criteria for using line in pencil drawings on pages 20–21 in the chapter on Line, including a photocopiable assessment sheet.

Self-evaluation

Internal self-evaluation

During the drawing process there is an internal conversation taking place; this is true whatever the age and ability of the artist. This dialogue helps to develop and refine the drawing.

Self-questioning appropriate to younger children might be along the lines of:
- How is this going?
- Am I pleased with it?
- What should I change?
- How am I going to change it?
- Is it finished?
- What is good / not so good about it?
- How does it look if I hold it away from myself a little?
- How would it look to someone else?
- How does it look on the paper?
- Have I placed it on the paper well?

This questioning can be developed by the teacher prompting the questions by saying, *'When you are drawing you should ask yourself ...'.* Suggest one or more of the questions above. In order to evaluate their work, children need to be given the vocabulary necessary to do this and possibly also a framework.

Spoken self-evaluation

Internal self-evaluation naturally leads on to being able to review what they have done and say what they think and feel about it.

Here the vocabulary may need to be modelled by teacher questioning.

In order for the children to be able to talk about their work the following questions could be asked:
- What are you most pleased about with this piece of work?
- What part do you think is most successful? (the composition, the use of media, the tones, textures, patterns, shapes)
- What did you find most difficult?
- What problems did you meet?
- How did you solve / not solve those problems?
- If you did it again is there anything you would change?
- How would you change it?
- If you had more time what would you do next?
- Are you proud of it?
- Would it look very different / better if you ... used different paper / media / changed the scale / looked at it from a distance / changed the colours?

Developing this kind of questioning will help children talk about their work and be able to make internal independent judgements as they mature.

Example of Resource sheet 13 completed by Anna Marie Searle, Year 2

Written evaluations

Written evaluations can take different forms.

Year 2 children and more able Year 1 children could annotate their work on the border or underneath, especially in their sketchbooks. For example:

> *'I am proud of this because it was hard to get the teddy to look furry and I think it does. I wish I had drawn it bigger.'*
>
> Jamie, age 7

Younger or less able children could have their annotations scribed for them.

Children could use a self-assessment frame such as the ones on Resource sheets 13 and 14 (pages 114 and 115). Resource sheet 13 is for Year 1 and less able Year 2 children. Resource sheet 14 is for Year 2 children. These are very useful at the end of a chapter, term or year. They can be pasted into sketchbooks and referred to at a later date. For example, *'Remember what you said you wanted to get better at this term. Look back in your sketchbooks and remind yourself of what you wrote.'*

The same kind of language can be used when writing comments in sketchbooks. For example, *'This is a careful, sensitive drawing. Were you pleased with it? Which part were you most pleased with?'* Or, *'I can see you had problems with this. What did you find most difficult? How would you do it differently if you did it again?'*

Children could be encouraged to look for teacher comments and questions in their sketchbooks and write a response if appropriate. They could also be encouraged to periodically look back through their sketchbooks to see if they think they are making progress, and write comments against their favourite piece of work. For example: *'I am really proud of this.'*

Peer evaluation

Children should be able to review the artwork of their peers and say what they think and feel about it. The same kind of language can be used for this as for self-evaluation. Children, however, need to learn to be sensitive to each other and to be 'critical friends'. They need to be able to trust each other and be thoughtful and supportive in their comments. In the early stages of developing peer evaluation they need to be confined to positive comments. Later, when trust has been built up and children are better able to express their responses using appropriate vocabulary, some supportive criticism can be introduced. Again this will need to be modelled. For example:

❏ What do you think Jade could do to this drawing to make it even better?
❏ What problems do you think Dan had with this drawing? How could he solve them?

The peer evaluation can be built into the lesson, and then used in the plenary or summing up at the end of the session. At appropriate points during the drawing lesson, ask children to stop drawing and take a walk around the classroom and have a look at each other's drawings. Tell them to do this in silence with no spoken comments. Ask them to look at each other's drawings and ask them to silently choose one drawing that they think is particularly good. Warn them that you will be asking why they chose it. (Potential pitfall! Children may choose friends' work.)

Question children about their choices:
❏ Which drawing do you think is really good?
❏ Why do you think it is good?
❏ What do you think of the way Holly has drawn the guinea-pig's fur (or whatever)? Here is a good opportunity to draw attention to other positive aspects of Holly's drawing. The first child could be asked if and how the drawing could be improved in any way. Then ask Holly to select a drawing that she thought was good and question her about the reasons for her choice.

Explain to them that artists get ideas from other artists and often talk to each other about their work.

Reporting and tracking progress

One way to keep track of progress is to collect sample drawings from the whole class biannually or termly. These can be annotated and kept in a file. Over a number of years this will give a record of each child's drawing development over their time in school.

Children's drawings tell a lot about children's maturity and something of their character.

The filed drawings are useful for planning and for reporting to parents.

The drawings must be collected in the same way each time and in the same circumstances. For example, children should be allocated the same time for each sample drawing (e.g. 10 minutes), be given the same medium (e.g. pencil), and the same subject matter (e.g. figure drawing), it will then be easier to compare drawings.

Drawings can be compared against the previous term's drawings and against the general standard of the year group.

Another way would be to take a sample of a figure drawing one term, a landscape the next term and a close observational drawing from the last term. These drawings can be annotated, with specific strengths or weaknesses noted and possible ways forward suggested. The class teacher or the art co-ordinator could keep the files.

Recording coverage of work

To check coverage of chapters, photocopy the relevant part of the contents list. Highlight the lessons covered, possibly making a written note beside the lessons of the programmes of study covered. These are to be found in the box at the top of each lesson page. The skills in this book cover all the programmes of study relating to drawing, evaluating and developing work.

A colour code could be used: green for covered satisfactorily, and red for lessons that were not successful for some reason. A note could be made by these for future reference.

To check for National Curriculum coverage, photocopy the programmes of study and highlight the ones that have been covered.

Both these records of coverage could be kept in a planning or records file.

If you are using the QCA schemes of work, the skills required could be taught prior to delivering the QCA unit. For example the QCA unit 1a *Self Portrait* could be taught after covering some of the lessons from the Figures and faces chapter. The units 2c *Mother Nature Builder* and 2c *Can Buildings Speak?* involve observational drawing so drawing and looking skills could be taught prior to the delivery of these units. This should result in a higher standard of final outcomes.

Reports

Here are some statements which might be useful when writing reports:

☐ Has acquired / is acquiring drawing skills after working in a range of media
☐ Draws well / is beginning to draw with great sensitivity to line and tone
☐ Has developed / is beginning to develop an understanding of pattern/tone/texture
☐ Demonstrates good drawing skills in all designing activities
☐ Is able to draw and talk about familiar objects
☐ Is able to talk about own work using appropriate vocabulary
☐ Is able to discuss own work and say what he / she might change or develop in the future
☐ Is developing good powers of observation
☐ Shows close attention to detail when drawing.

Less positive comments:
☐ Finds some aspects of this subject difficult but is working hard to improve skills
☐ Needs to be more willing to discuss a piece of work and how it might be improved
☐ Must avoid the tendency to rush, and spend a little more time looking and thinking carefully when drawing.

Glossary

Art pastels: Soft chalky pastels, quite smudgy.

Bleed/move: A term which describes what happens when a colour runs when wet or wetted.

Brusho: Powdered watercolour that can be sprinkled directly onto wet drawings, or made up with water as a thin paint. Usually comes in lovely bright colours but can be used for delicate or translucent colour.

Cartridge paper: Slightly rough paper of medium weight, ideal for drawing and painting, can be coloured.

Charcoal: Specially burned twigs used for drawing, comes in different thicknesses. Drawings usually need fixing, with fixative or hairspray.

Composition: The arrangement of elements in a picture.

Conté crayons (soft pastels): Drawing medium made from compressed coloured chalk, often in earth or landscape colours.

Contour: The edge as seen around the outside of a shape or form.

Cross-hatching: Form of shading created by crossed lines.

Elements: As referred to in the National Curriculum for Art and Design: line, tone, shape, form, pattern, colour, texture and space.

Etching: Type of printing, blocks usually made by acid eating into uncovered parts of metal plate. Plate is then inked and prints are taken.

Fixative: Spray used to prevent charcoal or chalky pastel drawings from further smudging. Can be purpose bought, but cheap unscented hairspray makes a good substitute. Fixative should always be used when children have left the room and will not be back for an hour or so, as some children may be sensitive to the fumes.

Foreground: Lower area of drawing representing the area nearest to viewer.

Form: The three-dimensional shape of something.

Graphite: Hard drawing medium, silvery lead colour.

Landscape: Paper alignment when paper is placed with shorter sides vertical.

Medium/media: Different drawing materials: pencil, charcoal, pen, etc.

Move/bleed: A term which describes what happens when a colour runs when wet or wetted.

Narrative drawing: A drawing which tells a story in some way, or a sequence of events.

Oil pastels: Slightly sticky pastels made from coloured chalk bound with oil. Colours blend well. Useful for creating scraper and wax-resist pictures.

Op Art: Short for optical art, pictures usually consisting of lines or shapes that create optical illusions. Often giving the illusion of movement.

Pattern: An image that is repeated in a regular fashion.

People crayons: Commercially produced crayons, usually sold in a pack, made up of colours for different skin, hair and eyes.

Portrait: Paper alignment when paper is placed with shorter sides horizontal.

Schema: A formulated drawing that children have arrived at which represents, say, a house, a tree or a person, which they then use every time to represent that subject, even when drawing from first-hand experience.

Single-hatching: A series of single lines, drawn close together to create an area of tone.

Surrealism: An art movement which uses realist images but puts them together in an unusual or dream-like way. Salvador Dali is a Surrealist artist.

Texture: In drawing, texture means creating the impression something has a surface feel to it.

Tone: Darkness or lightness of a colour (including gradual shades of black through to white).

Viewfinder: Piece of black card, plastic or paper with a shape cut out of the middle. This is used to look closely at areas of a drawing or artefact. Can be used as a frame, to help children to compose a picture. The centre shape can be round, oval, square, rectangular, to suit purpose.

Archie Muirhead, Year 1

100

Bibliography

Barnes, Rob. *Art, Design and Topic Work 8–13*, Routledge Taylor & Francis

Camp, Jeffrey. *Draw: How to Master the Art*, Dorling Kindersley

Capon, Robin. *Drawing Techniques*, The Crowood Press

Clement, Robert, and Page, Shirley. *Primary Art: Investigating and Making in Art*, Oliver & Boyd

Cole, Roger. *Drawing with Children*, Private publication

Cox, Maureen. *Children's Drawing*, Penguin Books

da Vinci, Leonardo et al. *A Treatise on Painting,* Dover Publications

Devon Curriculum Advice. *Planning, Evaluation and Assessment*, DCA

DfEE. *Art and Design National Curriculum*, Qualifications and Curriculum Authority

Dixon, Peter. *Standing Points*, Private publication

Dobson, Bert. *Keys to Drawing*, A&C Black

Edwards, Betty. *Drawing on the Right Side of the Brain*, Harper Collins

Elderfield, John. *The Drawings of Henri Matisse*, W W Norton

Foster, Patience. *Drawing*, Usbourne

Frank, Frederick. *The Zen of Seeing: Seeing Drawing as Meditation*, Random House

Gormley, Antony. *Drawing*, British Museum Press

Hayes, Colin. *The Complete Guide to Painting and Drawing Techniques and Materials*, Phaidon

Lemos, Pedro. *Applied Art*, Pacific Press Publishing Association

Mann, Ida, and Pirie, Antoinette. *The Science of Seeing*, Pelican Books

Mendelowitz, Daniel M. *Drawing: A Study Guide*, Holt Rinehart & Winston

Nicolaides, Kimon. *The Natural Way to Draw*, Andre Deutsch

Parramon, Joe. *The Complete Book of Drawing*, Phaidon

Robinson, Gillian. *Sketchbooks: Explore and Store*, Hodder Arnold

Sedgewick, Dawn and Fred. *Drawing to Learn*, Hodder Arnold

Simpson, Ian. *Drawing, Seeing and Observation*, A&C Black

van Gogh, Vincent. *The Letters* (translated by Arnold Pomerans), Penguin Classics

Welton, Jude. *Drawing: A Young Artist's Guide*, Dorling Kindersley

Williams, Geoffrey. *African Designs*, Dover Publications

Useful websites

www.aboriginalartonline.com
Australian Aboriginal Dreamtime images and stories.

www.accessart.org.uk
Useful information on drawing and children's interactive art activities.

www.artcyclopedia.com
Excellent access to galleries, museums and artists. Easy to search.

www.arteducation.com
Lesson plans on art topics. Includes step-by-step guidance with teacher's notes.

www.artteaching.co.uk
Has links to art galleries. Click on multicultural art for Aboriginal art, Hindu art, Islamic and Ancient Egyptian art.

www.davidmach.com
Website of British artist David Mach.

www.drawingpower.org.uk
Find out about the national campaign for drawing.

www.drumcroon.org.uk
For anyone interested in promoting education through art. Has links to other galleries.

www.google.co.uk
This is a brilliant search engine for images. Having opened up Google, click on 'images' and type in your request. Shows pages of related images.

www.metmuseum.org
Displays more than 3,500 works from New York's Metropolitan Museum, includes growing timeline of international developments in art.

www.moma.org
New York's monumental gallery of modern art.

www.mos.org/leonardo/index.html
Child-friendly site, easy access, lots of interesting information about Leonardo da Vinci. NB: Note his eyes following the cursor on the opening page!

www.nationalgallery.org.uk
The National Gallery website. Has an education section.

www.npg.org.uk
The National Portrait Gallery. An excellent resource, including an education department.

www.nsead.org
Website of the National Society for Education in Art and Design. Among other useful and up-to-date information about art education, has database of around 300 units of work.

www.tate.org.uk
The Tate gallery's website.

www.vangoghgallery.com
Lists and displays all van Gogh's drawings.

Bobo 'Do' masks in Burkina Faso. © Charles and Josette Lenars/CORBIS

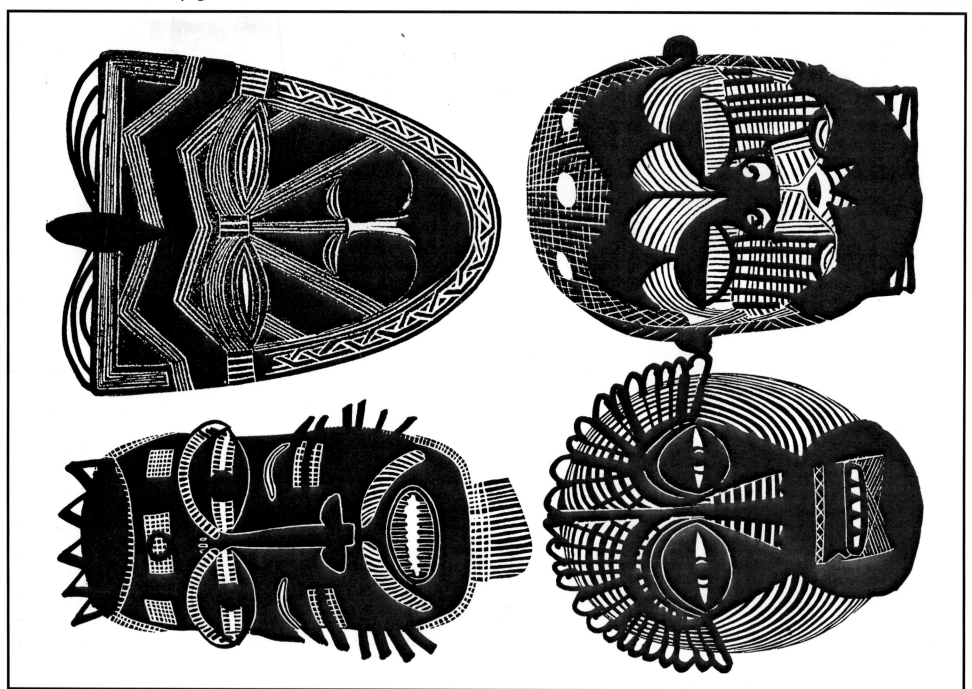

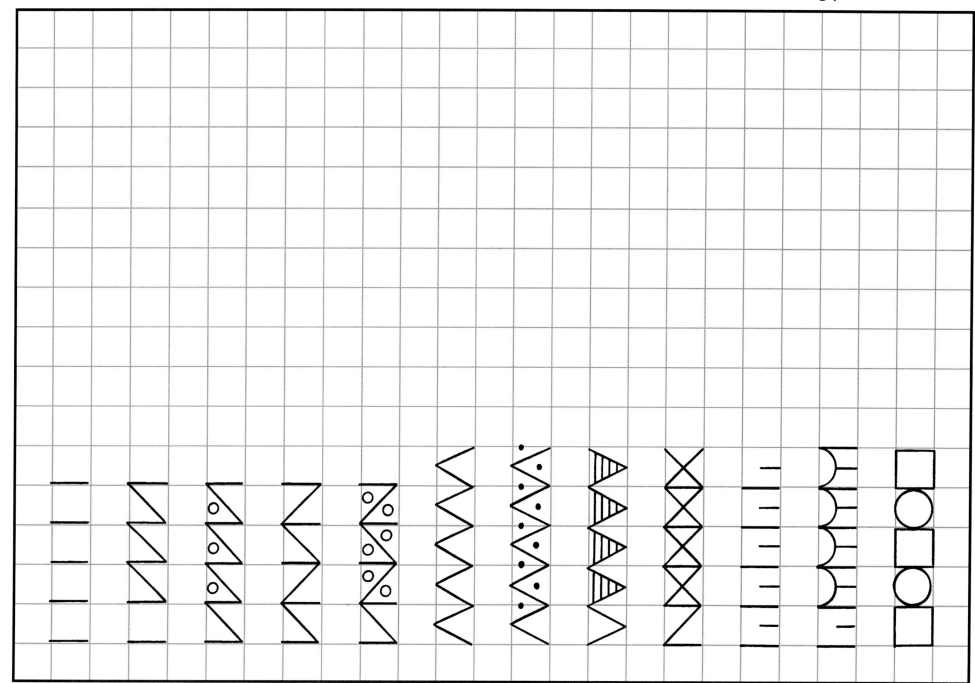

Handwriting patterns

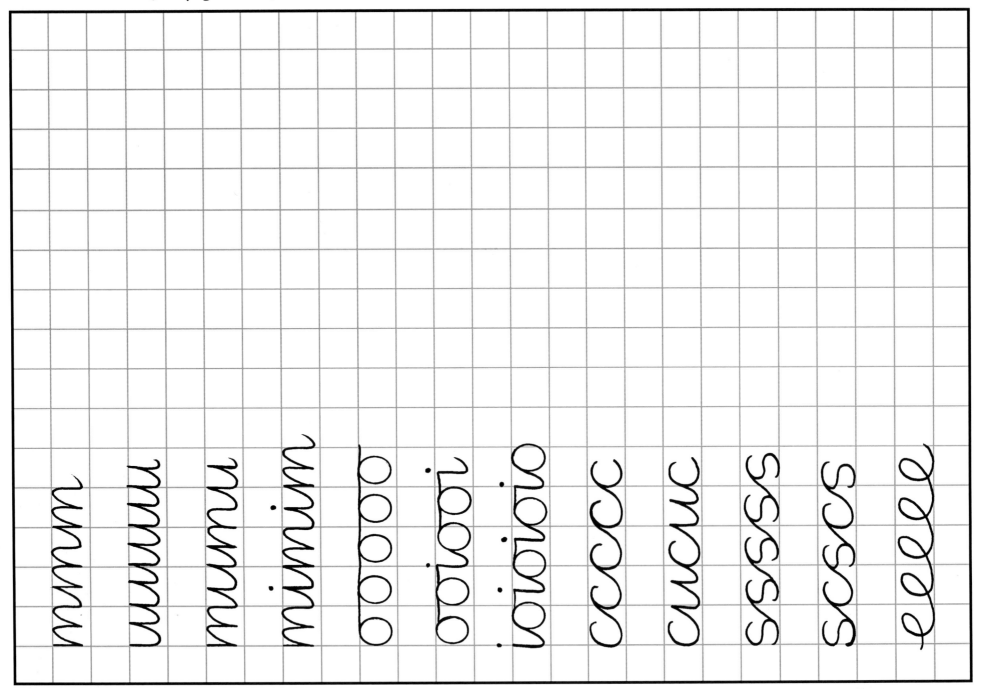

Making doodles

Start with a simple shape.

Add to it. You could use handwriting patterns and dots.

The doodle should grow slowly.
Draw as carefully as you can.

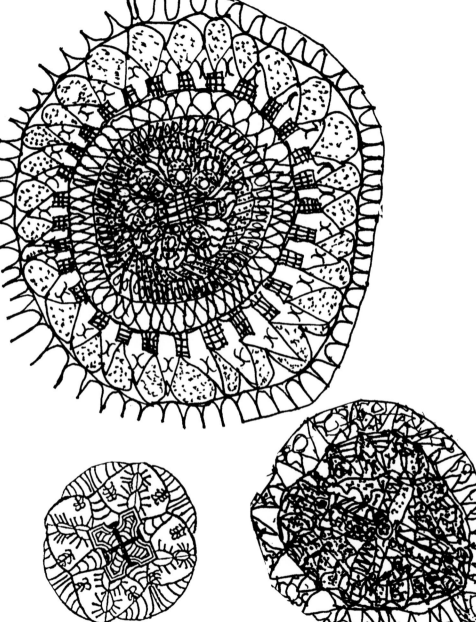

Pieter Bruegel, Children's Games, 1560

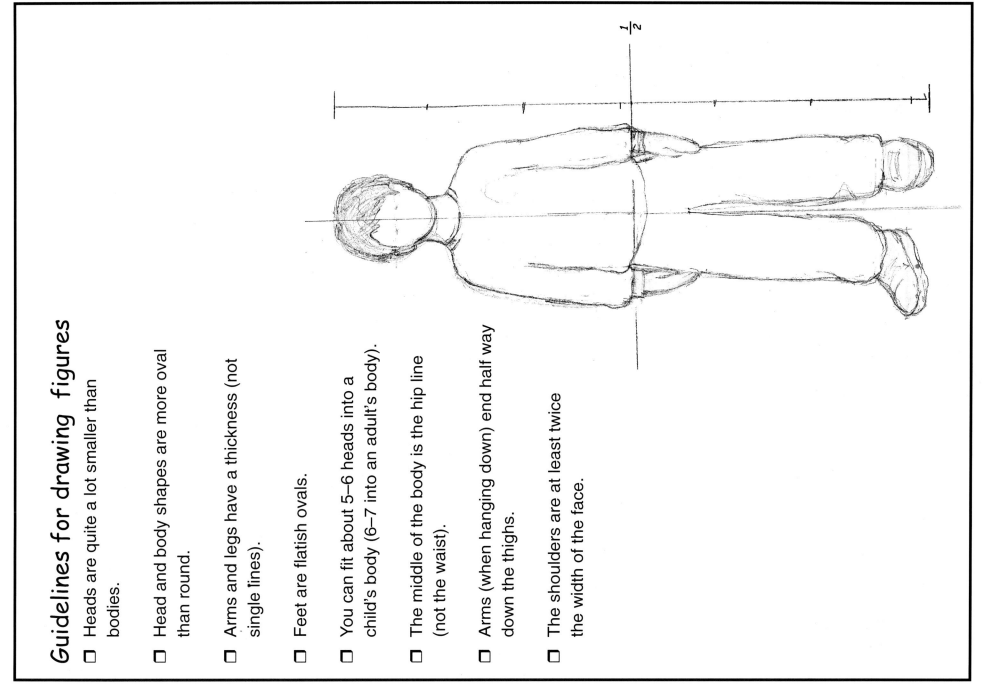

Guidelines for drawing figures

☐ Heads are quite a lot smaller than bodies.

☐ Head and body shapes are more oval than round.

☐ Arms and legs have a thickness (not single lines).

☐ Feet are flatish ovals.

☐ You can fit about 5–6 heads into a child's body (6–7 into an adult's body).

☐ The middle of the body is the hip line (not the waist).

☐ Arms (when hanging down) end half way down the thighs.

☐ The shoulders are at least twice the width of the face.

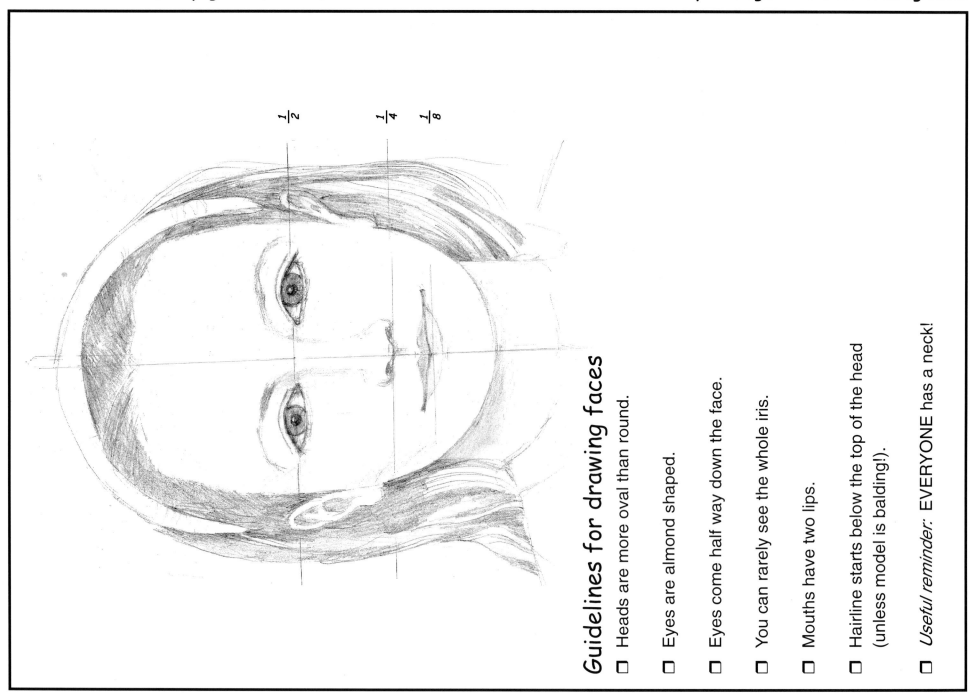

Guidelines for drawing faces

☐ Heads are more oval than round.

☐ Eyes are almond shaped.

☐ Eyes come half way down the face.

☐ You can rarely see the whole iris.

☐ Mouths have two lips.

☐ Hairline starts below the top of the head (unless model is balding!).

☐ *Useful reminder:* EVERYONE has a neck!

$\frac{1}{2}$ $\frac{1}{4}$ $\frac{1}{8}$

Drawing skills assessment list

Name:
Class:

Using media:
Draws using a range of marks with pencil
Draws in pen with confidence

Use of key elements
Uses a variety of lines
Includes tone
Tries to depict texture
Observes and draws patterns

Strategies
Uses light lines at outset of drawing

Observation
Looks carefully before and during drawing
Observes and includes detail

Composition
Places subject well on paper
Uses space well

Speaking and self-evaluating skills
Talks effectively about own drawings
Identifies areas for development
Talks about works of art using appropriate vocabulary

Attitude
Draws with confidence
Concentrates well

Colour coding
Green = excellent
Yellow = satisfactory
Red = problems

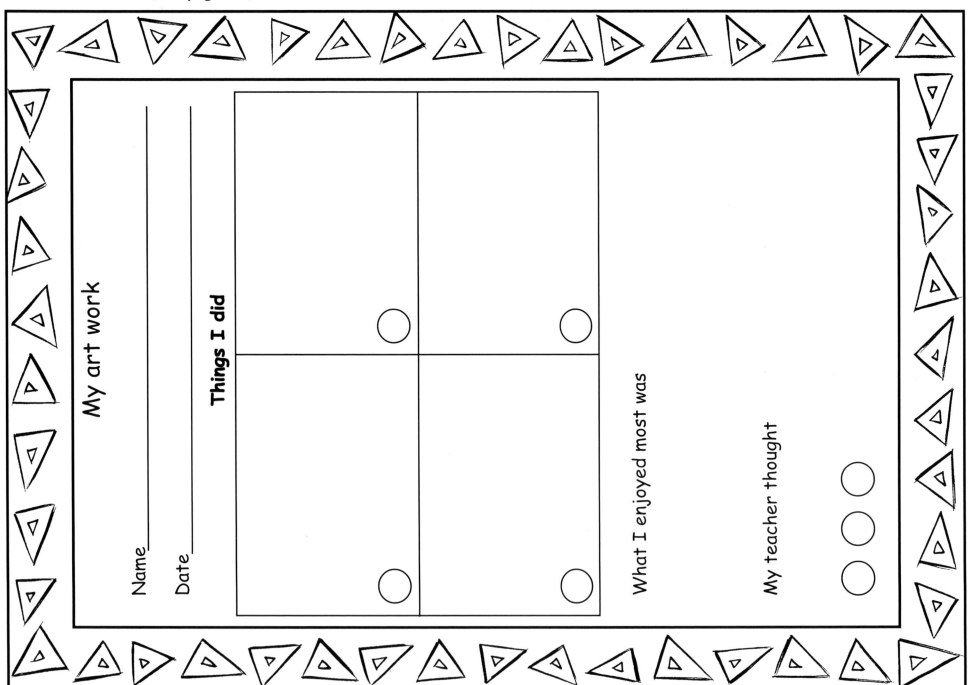

My art work

Name

Date

Things I did

What I enjoyed most was

My teacher thought

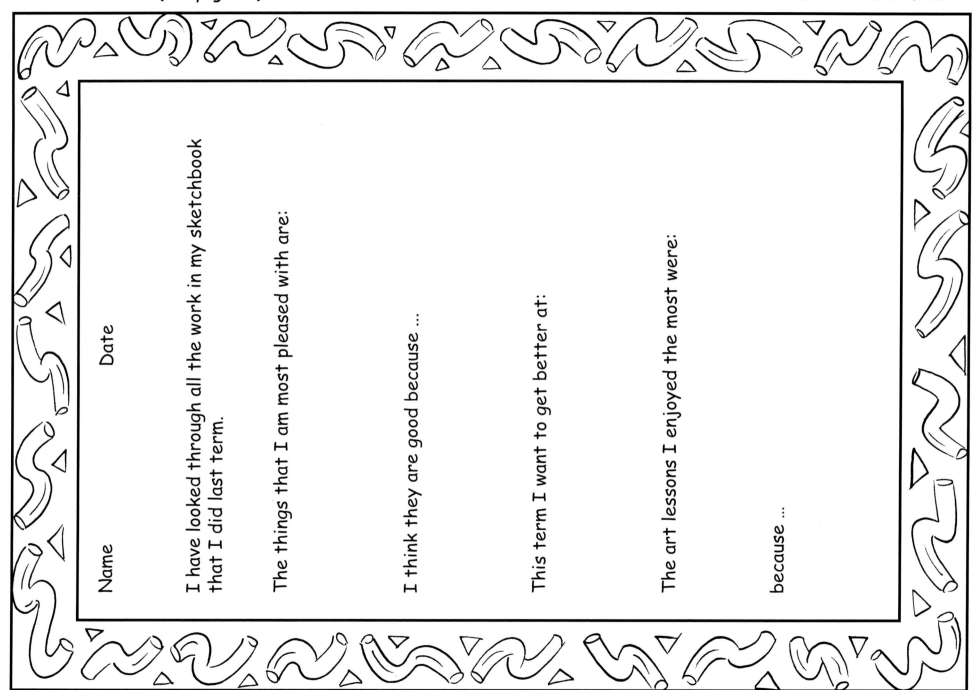

Name

Date

I have looked through all the work in my sketchbook
that I did last term.

The things that I am most pleased with are:

I think they are good because ...

This term I want to get better at:

The art lessons I enjoyed the most were:

because ...

Great art ideas for 3–12 year olds

Preschool Art
It's the Process, not the Product

With over 230 process-oriented, open-ended art experiences for children aged 3–6 in this book, you'll never be stuck for ideas.

Activities range from drawing, painting and sculpture to craft, collage and construction, including:

☐ Great goop ☐ Fingerpaint leaves ☐ Weaving board
☐ Corn-cob print ☐ Life-size animal ☐ Colourful stir sticks
☐ Towel chalk design ☐ Roller fence painting

Why not try something different?

The Big Messy* Art Book
*But Easy To Clean Up

Open the door for children to explore art on a grander, more expressive scale. Suitable for all ages.

Activities range from drawing, painting and sculpture to craft, collage and construction. Each activity is labelled to indicate experience level required, amount of mess produced, ease of preparation and planning and any safety issues.

Go beyond the ordinary and into the amazing!

Activities include:
☐ living pendulum art ☐ doormat prints ☐ drip and fold with a friend
☐ squeegee scraping ☐ streamers artwork ☐ hanging glue squiggles
☐ fly swatter painting and much more ...

Discovering Great Artists
Hands-on Art for Children in the Styles of the Great Masters

Help children to understand and experience artists' styles and techniques through their own artistic works. Over 100 innovative, fun and unique art activities. Suitable for children aged 4–12. More than 80 great masters are featured ranging from Leonardo da Vinci and Renoir to Escher and Grandma Moses.

Activities include:
☐ Michelangelo – Fresco Plaque ☐ Rembrandt – Shadowy Faces
☐ Degas – Resist in Motion ☐ Picasso – Fractured Friend
☐ Lichtenstein – Comic Dots

Creative Activities for the Early Years
Thematic Art and Music Activities

Creative Activities for the Early Years contains over 160 art and craft activities for use by reception classes, nurseries, playgroups and mother and toddler groups, as well as by parents and carers.

These tried and tested activities will help children to:
☐ Use their imagination
☐ Express themselves creatively
☐ Communicate their ideas
☐ Develop gross and fine motor skills

The activities are grouped by popular early years themes, together with songs and rhymes, suggestions for stories and things to talk about. Whether your topic is the autumn, the Chinese New Year, the coastline, or ourselves, you can be sure you and your children will find the variety of activities interesting and entertaining.